FALKIRK & DISTRICT ATI

C000049688

CONT

Key to Maps	2-3	Grangemouth			0-61
Avonbridge	51	Kirkliston			57
Banknock	44-45	Larbert	12-13	Skinflats	20-21
Bo'ness	24-26	Laurieston	66-67	Slamannan	54-55
Bonnybridge	46-49	Linlithgow	28-29	South Queensferry	32-33
Bridgend	30	Linlithgow Bridge	27	Stenhousemuir	12-13
Brightons	64-65	Maddiston	60-61	Torphichen	56
Broxburn	38-39	Newbridge	40-41	Uphall	36-37
California	58-59	Philpstoun	30	Wallacestone	58-59
Carron	14-15	Polmont	68-69	Westfield	51
Carronshore	14-15	Ratho	42-43	Westquarter	66-67
Denny	50	Ratho Station	40-41	Whitecross	52-53
Dunipace	50	Redding	66-67	Winchburgh	31
Falkirk	4-11	Reddingmuirhead	62-63	Index to Streets	70-77

KEY TO MAP SYMBOLS

M9	Motorway	P F A	Police / Fire / Ambulance station
A9	A road (dual / single)	▲	Primary school
B816	B road	▼	Secondary school
	Unclassified road	i	Tourist information centre
	Track / Footpath	P	Parking
	Railway	F	Filling station
	Notable building	H	Hospital
	Built-up area	PO	Post office
	Parks etc.	m	Museum
	Woodland	⌂	Caravan site
	Loch / Reservoir	✕	Battlefield
	River / Burn	+	Place of worship

ISBN 1 86097 086 9

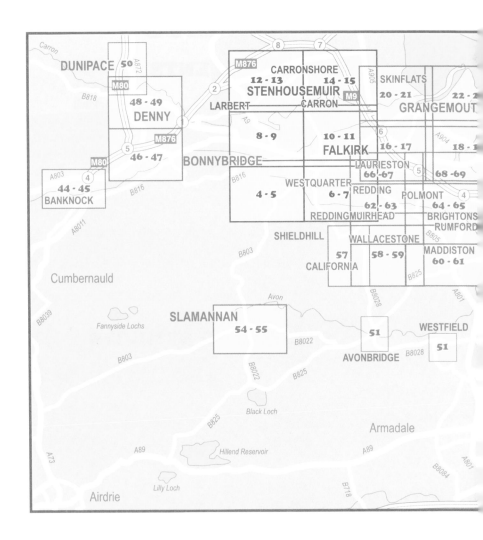

Note:

Pages shown on this diagram with blue frames and numbers correspond to those pages in the atlas with blue frames and page numbers. They are at a scale of 1:14,000.

Those shown with turquoise frames and numbers correspond to the pages in the atlas with turquoise frames and page numbers. They are at a scale of 1:12,000.

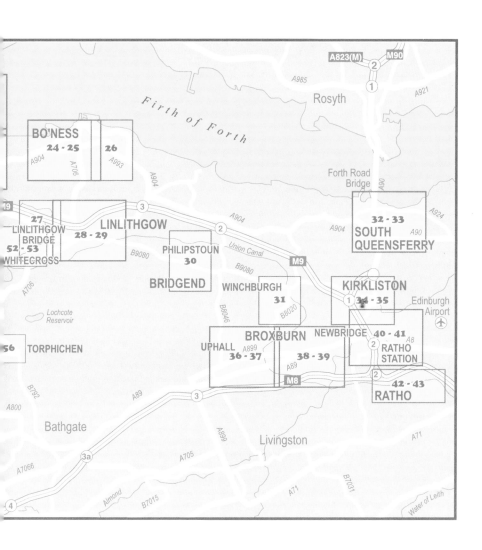

A823(M) M90

Rosyth

A985

A921

Firth of Forth

Forth Road
Bridge

BO'NESS
24 - 25   26
A904 A706 A993

A904

32 - 33
**SOUTH
QUEENSFERRY**
A904 A90

A924

19

27
LINLITHGOW
**LINLITHGOW
BRIDGE**
28 - 29

52 - 53

WHITECROSS

B9080

PHILIPSTOUN
30

BRIDGEND

Union Canal

B9080

M9

A706

Lochcote
Reservoir

WINCHBURGH
31

B8046

B6020

KIRKLISTON
1 34 - 35

Edinburgh
Airport

56 **TORPHICHEN**

BROXBURN

NEWBRIDGE 40 - 41

2 **RATHO
STATION**

A8

UPHALL A899
36 - 37

38 - 39

A89

M8

2

42 - 43
RATHO

B792

A89

3

A800

Bathgate

3a

A705

A899

Livingston

A71

A7066

A71

B7031

Almond

B7015

4

Water of Leith

4

A **B** **C** **D**

Park

Camelon

Clarinda Ave
Mariner St
Wilson Dr
Antonine Avenue
Fairlie Drive
Watling Drive
Watling Street

Kennard St
Glencairn St
Mossgiel St
Mariner Avenue
Wilson Avenue
Ross Cres
Glenfuir St

Ochiltree Terrace
FAIRLIE STREET

5

Forth and Clyde Canal

Camelon
Gens
Camelon Jnr FC

Antonine Gardens 1
Tamfourhill
Industrial Estate

Tamfourhill

Tamfourhill Avenue
Whitegates

Lime Road

TAMFOURHILL ROAD

B816

BONNYHILL ROAD

PO Brodick Pl
Antonine Wall

Rowan Crescent
Maryfield Pl
Lime Rd
Howie's Pl
Machrie Ct
CUMBRAE DRIVE

Kilbrennan Drive
Kintyre Pl
Carrick Pl
Davaar Pl
Arran Terr
Kinory Pl
Corrie Pl
Greenbank Pl

4

Carradale Avenue

B816
To Bonnybridge

S

Opencast

Workings

Roman Camp
(site of)

Greenbank Road

Tamfourhill
Wood

3

G
F

79

Canada
Wood

Greenrig
Strip

2

Craigburn
Wood

1

Craigieburn

85

A **B** 86 **C** **D**

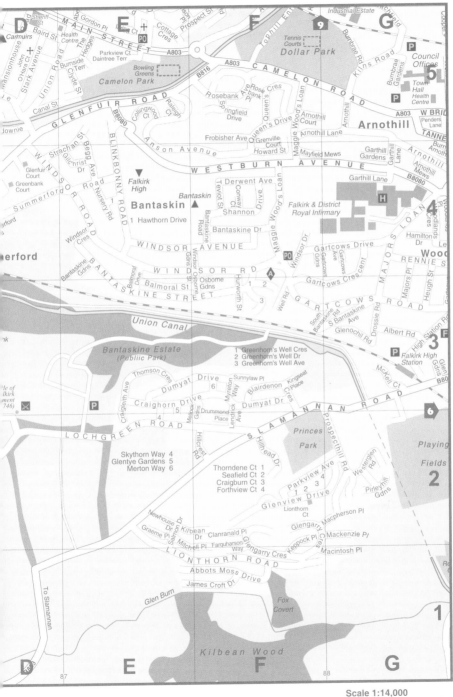

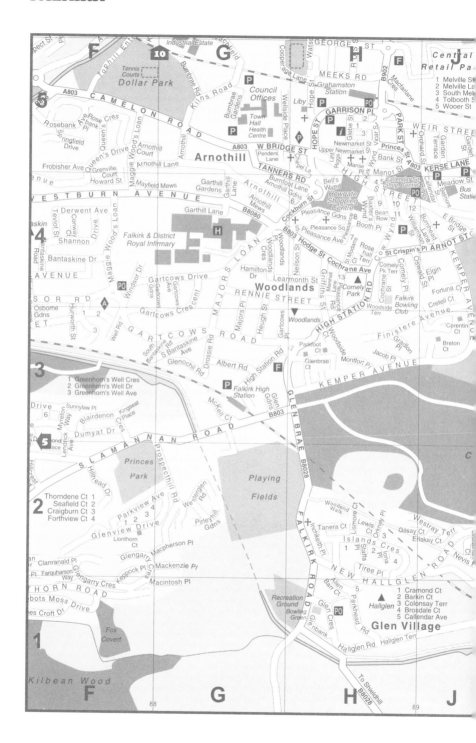

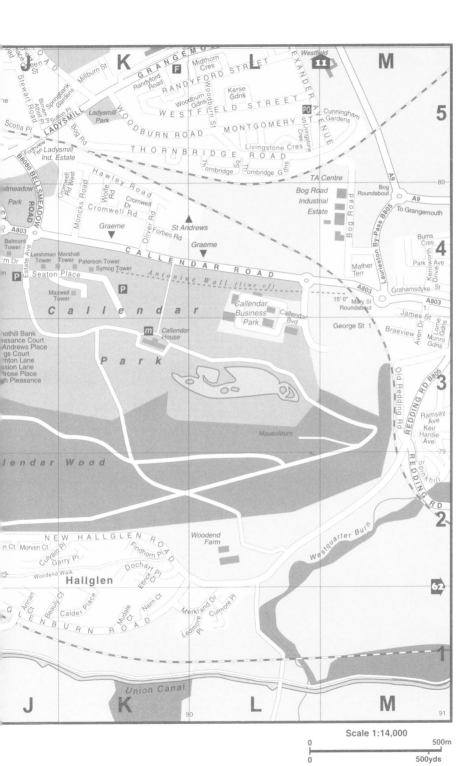

Scale 1:14,000

0   500m

0   500yds

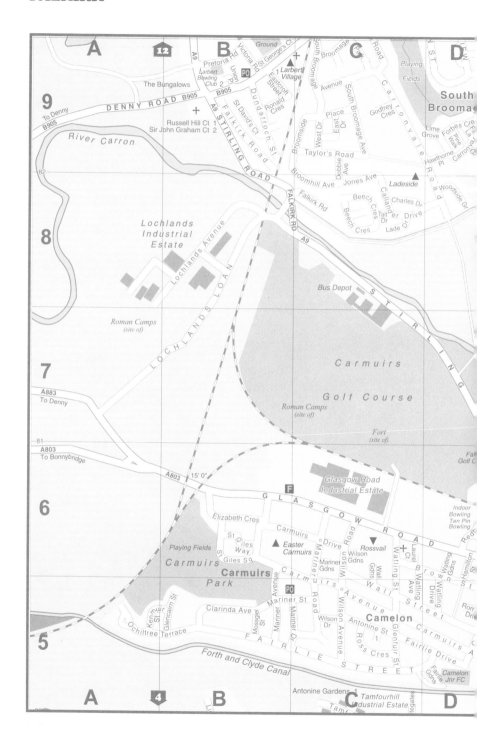

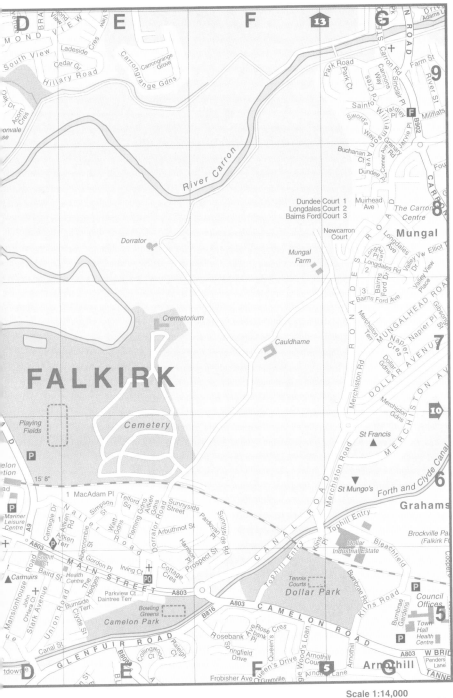

FALKIRK

Mungal

Scale 1:14,000

0   500m
0   500yds

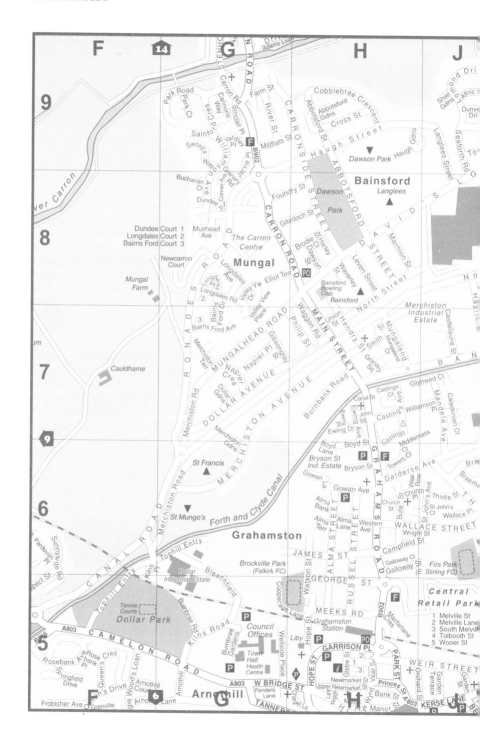

J K L M

15

Langlees

Bimam
Ct
Lomond Drive
Morar
Dr
Dunkeld
Strivens
Dr
orth Road
Ave
N

Sewage
Works

9

ABBOTS ROAD

To Edinburgh

M9

82

n
ks

8

Western Distributor Road

**Bankside
Industrial
Estate**

Castle Road

Castle
Dr

Castle Cres

Castle
Ct

Castle
Ct

Castle Road

S I D E

STOBBS ROAD

West Mains
Industrial
Estate

West Mains Rd

The Roundel

Almond Rd

Almond Ct

Abbots Ct

7

Etna Ct

**Middlefield
Industrial
Estate**

Universal Road

E T N A   R O A D

Crescent

Hazel Gr

College

Burnfield
Place

Castings Road

Castings
Ct

Forbes
Ct

81

A904

To M9 & Grangemouth

Drive

York Street

Corrie
Court

Castings Road

MIDDLEFIELD ROAD

York
Dr

Kennard Street

Adam Street

Argyll Ave

Bruce St

Thornhill
Court

Grange
Dr

Grange Drive

King St

Victoria

▲

Middlefield

*Falkirk College
of Further & Higher
Education*

6

Westfield
Roundabout

A904

A9

Victoria
Park

PO

X

Fairfield
Place
Queen
St

Stewart Road

Westfield
Farm

16

GRANGEMOUTH ROAD

F

ALEXANDER AVENUE

Millburn St

Randyford
Road

RANDYFORD STREET

F

Midthorn
Cres

Kerse
Gdns

Woodburn
Gdns

Woodburn St

WESTFIELD STREET

PO

Cunningham
Gardens

Springbank
Gardens

Balbeam
Pl
Sutton Pl
Athol Pl

LADYSMILL

Ladysmill
Park

WOODBURN ROAD

Bog Rd

MONTGOMERY ST

Livingstone
Cres

5

Scotia Pl

Fortview
Ten
Ladysmill
Ind. Estate

THORNBRIDGE ROAD

Livingstone Cres

B8045

SEL

well
West

Hawley

J K L M

Thornbridge
Sq

Thornbridge Gdns

7

TA Centre

80

Scale 1:14,000

0 ————————————— 500m

0 ————————————— 500yds

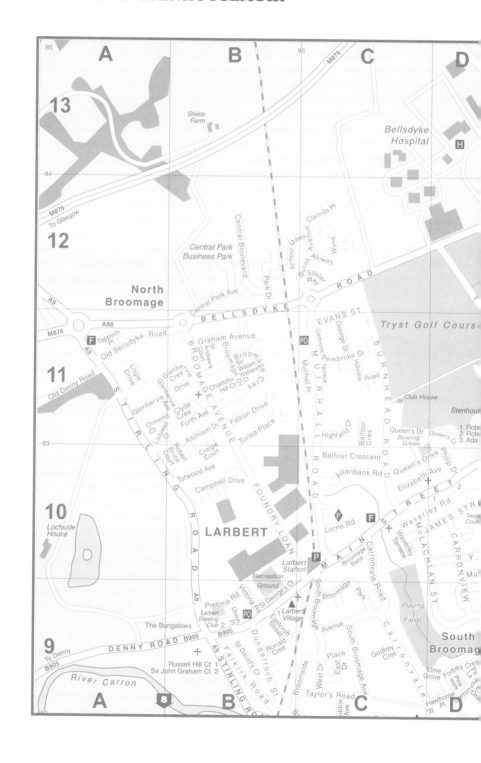

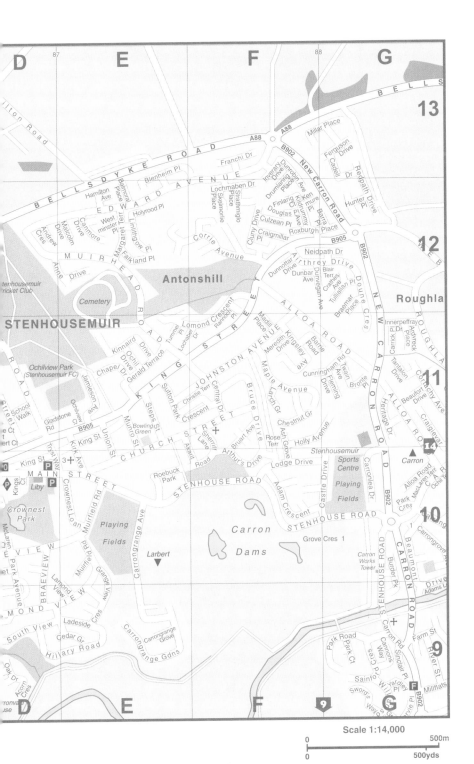

D 87 E F 88 G

13

BELLS

B E L L S

Hilton Road

BELLSDYKE ROAD

A88

A88

B902

New Carron Road

NEW CARRON ROAD

Millar Place

Ferguson Drive

Cadell Dr

Redpath Drive

Hunter Pl

Franchi Dr

Blenheim Pl

Hamilton Ave

Balmoral Place

Margaret Terr

EDWARD AVENUE

Lochmaben Dr

Strathmiglo Place

Skelmorlie Place

Inverary Drive

Dumdoin Drive

Drumlanrig Place

Finlarig Pl

Ken Ct

Kildrummy

Barra

Kilsyth Ave

Hunter Pl

Andrew Cres

Malcolm Drive

West minster Pl

Canmore Drive

Holyrood Pl

Tinlinlow Pl

Cluny Drive

Culzean Pl

Douglas Pl

Craigmillar Pl

Roxburgh Place

MUIRHEAD

Anne Drive

Falkland Pl

Corrie Avenue

Neidpath Dr

Airthrey Drive

Doune Cres

B902

ROAD

Antonshill

Dunnottar Drive

Dunbar Ave

Blair Terr

Crathes Ave

Tulliallan Pl

Braemar Place

Roughla

tenhousemuir ricket Club

Cemetery

STENHOUSEMUIR

Lomond Crescent

Ramloch Pl

KING STREET

Madill Place

Barre Road

ALLOA ROAD

Roughla

Innerpeffray Pl

Carrick Pl Dr

Ardvreck Place

ROUGHLA

Kinnaird Drive

Ochil Drive

Tummel

Lochaber Dr

JOHNSTON AVENUE

Meredith Dr

Kingsley Ave

Cunningham Rd

Fleming

Twain

Bronte

Tantalon Drive

Corrachy Ave

11

Ochilview Park (Stenhousemuir FC)

Jameson Av

Chapel Dr

Gerald Terrace

Christie Terr

Central Dr

Crescent

Maple Avenue

Larch Gr

Chestnut Gr

Ash Grove

Holly Avenue

Beaufort Drive

Craigleva

14

School

Walk

Ochilview Rd

Steps Ct

Sutton Park

STREET

Bruce Drive

Bruart Ave

Rose Terr

Stenhousemuir

Sports Centre

Carron

Craigleva

Carronlea Dr

Ochil Te

e Ct rt Ct

Gladstone Rd

B905

King St

Union St

Munro St

CHURCH

St Abait

Sheriff Lane

Arthur's Drive

Lodge Drive

Playing Fields

Castle Drive

Heritage Dr

Alloa Road

MacLaren Terr

Park Cres

0

King St

Tryst Way

3

MAIN

STREET

Crownest Loan

Roebuck Park

STENHOUSE ROAD

Adam Crescent

STENHOUSE ROAD

B902

CARRON ROAD

Beaumont Drive

Carrongrove

10

Kings Ct

Liby

P

Crownest Park

Muirfield Rd

Carrongrange Ave

Playing Fields

Carron Dams

Grove Cres 1

Carron Works Tower

Burder Pk

Park

Adams L

STENHOUSE ROAD

STENHOUSE ROAD

E VIEW

Mclaren Park Avenue

BRAEVIEW

Muirfield Pl

Muirfield Rd

Grange View

Larbert

Drive

Adams L

Farm Ct

MOND VIEW

South View

Ladeside

Cedar Gr

Lamond View

Carrongrange Grove

Carrongrange Gdns

Park Road

Park Ct

Carron Rd

Sinclair Dr

Cannons Way

River St

9

Oak Dr

Acorn Cres

Hillary Road

ronva

se

D E F 9 G B902

Millflats

Sainto

W Yardley

Swords

Way

Pl

F

Scale 1:14,000

0   500m

0   500yds

15

J   K   90   L   A905
To Kincardine,
Airth & Stirling   M   91

13

84

Kirkton

12

Brackenlees Rd

20

Bothkennar

Westertown
BOTHKENNAR ROAD

Skinflats   PO

Potter Pl
Coronation Pl   Zetland Pl   **11**

Westerton Terr

ore
NORTH MAIN STREET

ndship
lds

enue   Backrow   Newton Ave
Cample Terr
Edward Pl
The   Avenue   Binnie Pl   83

Church St
Waddell St
Dock St   Carron
House

Inglis Dr
Wardlaw Pl   **10**

River Carron   Yonderhaugh

To Grangemouth A905

Birnam
Ct
Morat
Dr
Dunkeld
Striven
Dr   Langlees   **9**

orth Road
t
Ave   ABBOTS ROAD

N   J   K   L   Sewage
Works   11   M   82

Scale 1:14,000

0   500m
0   500yds

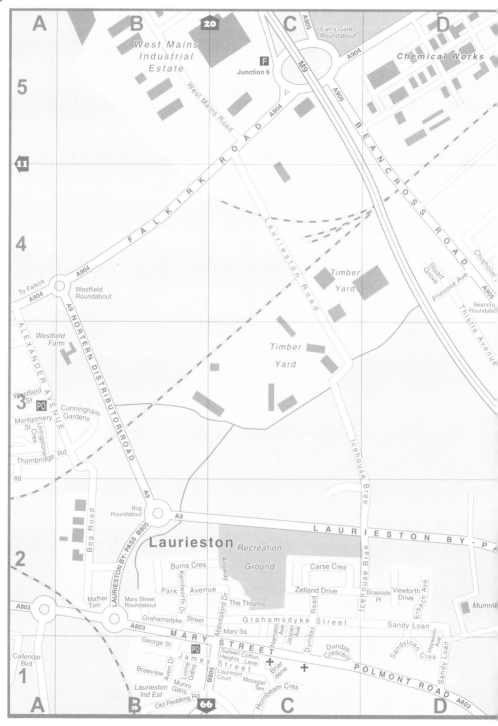

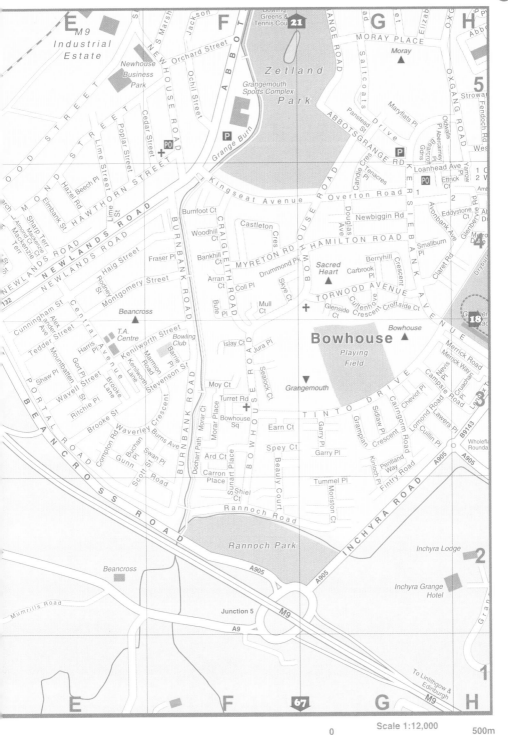

17

E
M9
Industrial
Estate

Newhouse
Business
Park

21

Bowling
Greens &
Tennis Cour

F

Jackson

Orchard Street

Ochil Street

ABBOT

Z e t l a n d

Grangemouth
Sports Complex

Park

MORAY PLACE

Moray

G

Saltcoats

Drive

H

Abb

5

OXGANG ROAD

Strowar
Fendoch Rd
Wes

NEWHOUSE ROAD

Cedar Street

Poplar Street

Lime Street

Grange Burn

ABBOTSGRANGE RD

Panstead St.

Marylhats Pl

Loanhead Ave
PO
Ettrick

Yarow

Oldwalls
Pl
Abercalmey
Bedgroft
Gdns

1 C
2 V
Amb

HAWTHORN STREET

P

Kingseat Avenue

Candle Pl

Cres Tenacres

Overton Road

KERSIEBANK

Eddystone
Ct

Avonbank Ave

Glenberve

Metro
Dr e

NEWLANDS ROAD

NEWLANDS ROAD

Hazel Rd
Beech Rd
Elmbank St

Sharp Terr
Jamond
Mackenzie
Terr

Haig Street

Montgomery Street

Fraser Pl

BURNBANK ROAD

CRAIGLEITH ROAD

Burnfoot Ct

Woodhill
Ct

Bankhill
Ct

Castleton

Cres

MYRETON RD

Drummond Pk

Arran
Ct

Coll Pl

Skye Ct

BOWHOUSE ROAD

HAMILTON ROAD

Douglas
Ave

Newbiggin Rd

Smallburn
Pl

Claret Rd

4

Sacred
Heart

Carbrook
Pl

Berryhill

Crescent

TORWOOD AVENUE

18

132

Cunningham St

Alex
ander
Ave

Tedder Street

Central Avenue

Beancross

T.A.
Centre

Kenilworth Street

Bowling
Club

Islay Ct

Jura Pl

Bute
Pl

Mull
Ct

Glenside
Ct

Cultenho
Crescent

Croftside Ct

Bowhouse

Bowhouse

AVENUE

5

Harris
Pl

Gort Pl

Mountbatten

Marmion
Road

Barrie
Lane

Stevenson St

Moy Ct

Sealock Ct

Bowhouse
Playing
Field

Merrick Road

Merrick Way

Nevis
Pl

Campsie Road

Lagy Ex

Shaw St

Wavell St

Ritchie St

Brooke
Lane

Brooke St

Waverley Crescent

Burns Ave

BURNBANK ROAD

Morar Ct

Turret Rd

Bowhouse
Sq

BOWHOUSE ROAD

TINTO DRIVE

Grampian

Sidlaw Pl

Cairngorm Road

Cheviot Pl

Lomond Road

Cuillin Pl

Lawers Pl

Cruachan

3

Grangemouth

Earn Ct

Garry Pl

Crescent

B9143

Compton Rd

Buchan

Gunn

Swan Pl

Scott Road

Dochart Path

Morar Place

Ard Ct

Carron
Place

Sunart Place

Beauly Court

Spey Ct

Garry Pl

Kinloch Pl

Pentland
Way

Fintry Road

Wholefla
Rounda

A905

A905

BEANCROSS ROAD

Shiel
Ct

Rannoch Road

Tummel Pl

Monston Ct

Mumills Road

Beancross

Rannoch Park

A905

A905

INCHYRA ROAD

Inchyra Lodge

Inchyra Grange
Hotel

Gran

2

Junction 5

M9

A9

To Linlithgow &
Edinburgh

M9

1

E

F

67

G

H

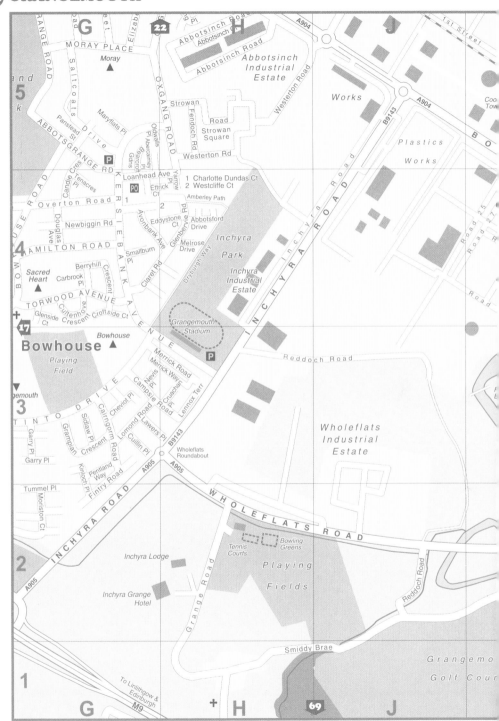

K   Tenacres   L   Bea   23   Avon Rd   M   N

5

Chemical
Works

Road 7   Road 9   Road 11

Road 6   Road 10

SS ROAD   Road   Road 24   ical   ks   2/a d   0 B   Sewage
Works

81

4

Road 31   Road 30C   Road 30   33   28

Buchan Rd   Ninian Rd   6th Street

4th Street   5th Street   Balmoral
Rd

3rd Street   Magnus Road   Bravo
St   7th Street

River Avon   Brae Rd   Alpha St   Bruce Rd

2nd Street   Magnus Road

Forties Road   Miller Road

Riverside Road   Compressor
House Road   East Road

ROAD 33   Quench Road   South Road   Flare Rd   GRANGEMOUTH ROAD A904   3

To Bo'ness

Works   Inveravon
Roundabout   A904   GRANGEMOUTH RD   A904

A905

80

WHOLEFLATS ROAD

Jinkabout Road   2

Ski Slope   Avondale Road

Club House   1

K   95   L   M   96   N

Scale 1:12,000
0   500m
0   500yds

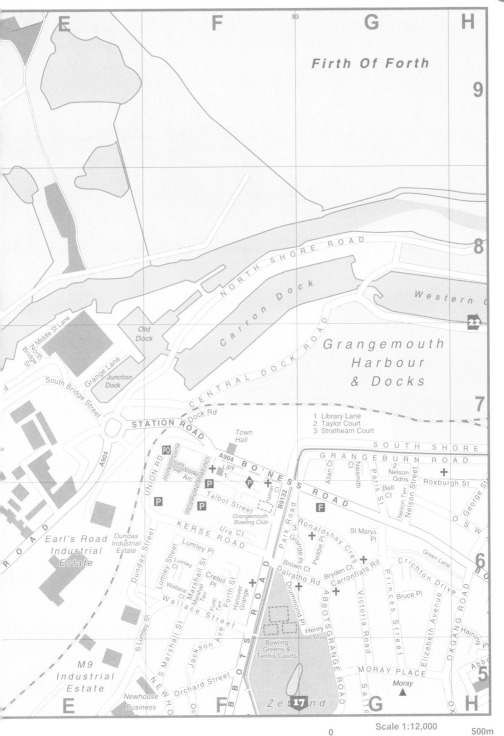

21

Firth Of Forth

9

North Shore Road

Carron Dock

Old Dock

Western

8

22

Grangemouth Harbour & Docks

Middle St Lane
North Bridge St
Grange Lane
Junction Dock
South Bridge Street

Central Dock Road

Dock Rd

7

STATION ROAD

Town Hall

1 Library Lane
2 Taylor Court
3 Strathearn Court

SOUTH SHORE

GRANGEBURN ROAD

Allan Ct
Nalsmith Ct
Nelson Gdns
Bell Ct
Nelson Terr
Nelson Street
Roxburgh St

George St

OSW

PO

UNION RD

A904

York Lane
York Sq
York Arc

La Porte Precinct
Liby 1
Palmer Ct

B9132

BO'NESS ROAD

Paris St

Talbot Street

Grangemouth Bowling Club

Ure Ct

F

Ronaldshay Cres

St Marys Pl

Green Lane

Crichton Drive

BO

6

KERSE ROAD

Lumley Pl

Brown Ct
Grange Rd
Peddie Rd
Bryden Ct
Carronflats Rd

Bruce Pl

Princes Street

Elizabeth Avenue

OXGANG ROAD

Haining Pl

Earl's Road Industrial Estate

Dundas Industrial Estate

Dundas Street

Lumley Street
Lumley Ct
Marshall Terr
Marshall St
Creteil St
Forth St
Hanover Grange

Wallace Ter
Wallace Street

Dalratho Rd
Drummond Pl

Victoria Road

Abb

H

5

M9 Industrial Estate

S Lumley St
S N S Marshall St
Jackson Ave
N Orchard Street

ABBOTS ROAD

Henry St

ABBOTSGRANGE ROAD

Sal

MORAY PLACE

Moray

OX

Newhouse Business

Bowling Greens & Tennis Courts

Zetland

17

E   F   G   H

Scale 1:12,000

0 ————————————— 500m
0 ————————————— 500yds

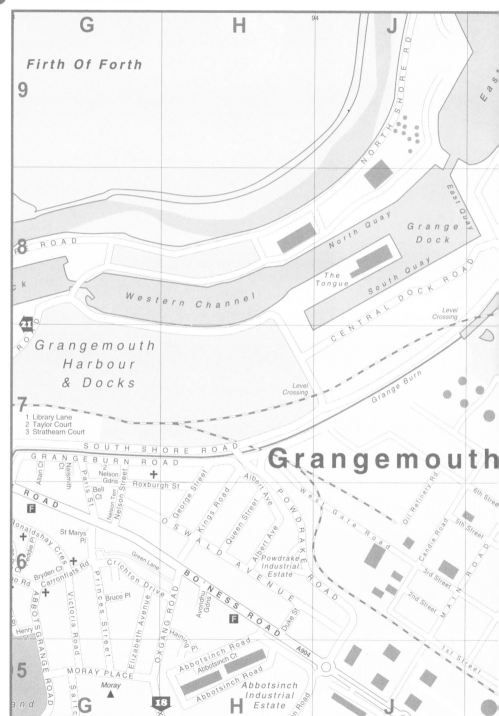

G **H** 94 **J**

Firth Of Forth

9

East

NORTH SHORE RD

East Quay

ROAD

8

North Quay

Grange Dock

ck

The Tongue

South Quay

CENTRAL DOCK ROAD

Level Crossing

Western Channel

ROAD

21

Grangemouth Harbour & Docks

Level Crossing

Grange Burn

7

1 Library Lane
2 Taylor Court
3 Strathearn Court

SOUTH SHORE ROAD

Grangemouth

GRANGEBURN ROAD

Allan Ct

Naismith Ct

2 Nelson Gdns

Roxburgh St

George Street

Kings Road

Albert Ave

Queen Street

Albert Ave

POWDRAKE

West Gate Road

Oil Refinery Rd

6th Street

5th Street

ROAD

Paris St

Bell Ct

Nelson Terr

Nelson Street

Candie Road

F

Ronaldshay Cres

St Marys Pl

Green Lane

Powdrake Industrial Estate

3rd Street

ROAD

MAIN

6

Eddie Rd

Bryden Ct

Carronflats Rd

Crichton Drive

Princes Street

OSWALD

2nd Street

no Rd

Bruce Pl

BO-NESS ROAD

AVENUE

Duke St

Henry St

ABBOTSGRANGE ROAD

Victoria Road

Elizabeth Avenue

OXGANG ROAD

Avondhu Gdns

Haining Pl

F

A904

1st Street

5

Saltc

MORAY PLACE

Moray ▲

18

Abbotsinch Road

Abbotsinch Ct

Abbotsinch Road

Abbotsinch Industrial Estate

n Road

and

G **H** **J**

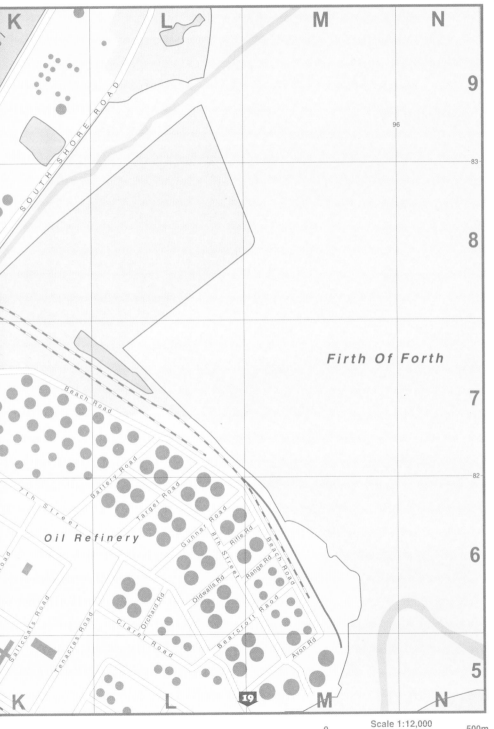

K   L   M   N

9

96

83

8

Firth Of Forth

7

82

SOUTH SHORE ROAD

Beach Road

Ballery Road

Target Road

Gunner Road

Rifle Rd

8th Street

Range Rd

Beach Road

Oldwalls Rd

Rd

Beatcroft Road

Avon Rd

Orchard Rd

Claret Road

Tenacres Road

Saltcoats Road

7th Street

Oil Refinery

6

5

K   L   19   M   N

Scale 1:12,000

0   500m
0   500yds

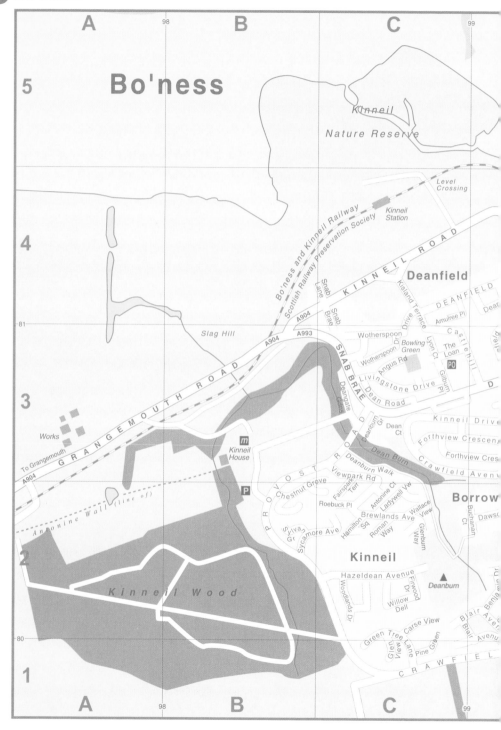

Bo'ness

5

Kinneil
Nature Reserve

Level
Crossing

Bo'ness and Kinneil Railway
Scottish Railway Preservation Society

Kinneil
Station

KINNEIL ROAD

4

Deanfield

DEANFIELD

Amulree Pl   Dean

Snab Lane

Snab Brae

Wotherspoon

A904

Castlehill

Slag Hill

A904   A993

Bowling
Green

Lyon Ct

The
Loan

PO

Di
Wotherspoon

Angus Rd

Livingstone Drive

SNAB BRAE

Dean Road

D

81

GRANGEMOUTH ROAD

Deangate Gdns

Dean
Ct

Kinneil Drive

3

Works

Kinneil
House

Provost Rd

Dean
Gr

Forthview Crescen

Forthview Cres

To Grangemouth

A904

Antonine Wall (line of)

Dean Burn

Deanburn Walk

Crawfield Aven

Viewpark Rd

Fairspark Terr

Antonine Ct

Ladywell Vw

Wallace
View

Borrow

P

Chestnut Grove

Roebuck Pl

Brewlands Ave

Roman
Way

Glenburn
Way

Buchanan
Ct

Dawso

Hamilton
Sq

Sycamore Ave

Sylvan
Gr

Kinneil

2

Hazeldean Avenue

Deanburn

Blair Benja

Blair Ave

80

Kinneil Wood

Woodlands Dr

Firwood
Dr

Willow
Dell

Green Tree Lane

Carse View

View

Pine Green

Blair
Avenu

1

CRAWFIEL

A   98   B   C   99

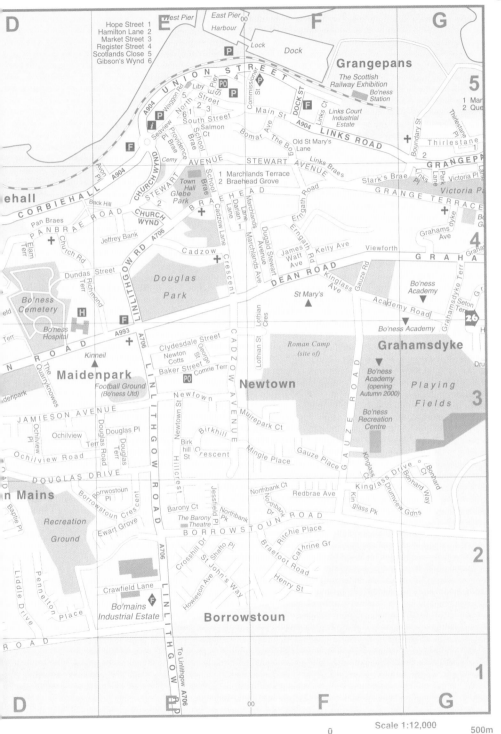

Hope Street 1
Hamilton Lane 2
Market Street 3
Register Street 4
Scotlands Close 5
Gibson's Wynd 6

West Pier
East Pier
Harbour
Lock
Dock

Grangepans

The Scottish
Railway Exhibition
Bo'ness
Station

5

1 Mar
2 Que

UNION STREET

A904

Waggon Rd
Seaview

North
Street
Liby
W Pier St
Commissioner St
PO
Main St
DOCK ST
Links Ct
Links Court
Industrial
Estate

LINKS ROAD

A904

South Street

Salmon
Ct

Bomar
The Bog
Old St Mary's
Lane

Links Braes

Boundary St

Thirlestane Pl
Thirlestane

GRANGEPA

GRANGE

School
Brae
Providence
Brae
Cemy

STEWART
AVENUE
STEWART AVENUE

1 Marchlands Terrace
2 Braehead Grove

Stark's Brae

Victoria Pl

GRANGE TERRACE

Victoria Pa

Bo

Town
Hall

Glebe
Park

BRAEHEAD

Cadzow Lane
Darian
Lane
Marchlands
Lane

Erngath Road

Erngath Rd
Dugald Stewart
Avenue

James
Watt
Ave

Kelty Ave

Viewforth

Grahams
Ave

GRAHA

Grah

Back Hill

CORBIEHALL

ehall

Pan Braes

PANBRAE ROAD

Elam
Terr

Church Rd

Jeffrey Bank

CHURCH
WYND

Marchlands
Avenue

DEAN ROAD

St Mary's

GRA

Cadzow

Crescent

Bo'ness
Academy

Grahamsdyke Terr

Seton
Terr

4

Dundas
Street

Richmond
Terr

Douglas

Park

Lothian
Cres

Kinglass
Ave

Gauze Rd

Academy Road

Bo'ness Academy

26

H

Bo'ness
Cemetery

Bo'ness
Hospital

A993

A706

LINLITHGOW RD

CHURCH ROAD

STEWART

A706

Kinneil

Clydesdale Street

Newton
Cotts
George

St
Comrie Terr

Baker Street

PO

Lothian St

Roman Camp
(site of)

GAUZE ROAD

Grahamsdyke

Bo'ness
Academy
(opening
Autumn 2000)

Bo'ness
Recreation
Centre

Playing

Fields

3

N ROAD

The Quarryknowes

Maidenpark

JAMIESON AVENUE

Football Ground
(Bo'ness Utd)

Newtown

Ochilview
Pl

Ochilview

Terr
Douglas Pl
Douglas Road

Douglas
Terr

Ochilview Road

DOUGLAS DRIVE

Newtown

St

Hillcrest

Birkhill

Birk
hill
St
Crescent

Newtown

Muirepark Ct

Mingle Place

Gauze Place

Newtown

LINLITHGOW ROAD

Kinglass

Kinglass Drive

Drumview Gdns

Bomhard
Ct
Bomhard Way

Drumview

2

n Mains

Recreation

Ground

Borrowstoun
Pl

Borrowstoun Cres

Ewart Grove

Barony Ct

The Barony
Theatre

Jessfield Pl

Northbank
Pk

Northbank
Dr

Northbank Ct

BORROWSTOUN ROAD

Redbrae Ave

Ritchie Place

Cathrine Gr

Kinglass Pk

Kinglass

Baglie Pl

Liddle Drive

Pennelton
Place

A706

Crosshill Dr

St Shafto Pl

St John's Way

Howeson Ave

Braefoot Road

Henry St

Crawfield Lane

Bo'mains
Industrial Estate

Borrowstoun

LINLITHGOW RD A706

To Linlithgow A706

ROAD

D   E   F   G

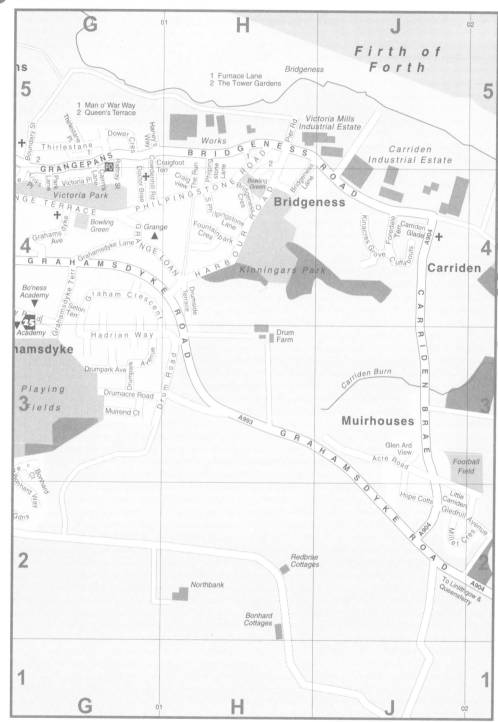

G 01 H J 02

Firth of Forth

5 5

1 Furnace Lane
2 The Tower Gardens

Bridgeness

1 Man o' War Way
2 Queen's Terrace

Dower Cres

Thirlestane

GRANGEPANS

Works

B R I D G E N E S S

Victoria Mills
Industrial Estate

Carriden
Industrial Estate

Victoria Pl

Victoria Park

Craigfoot
Terr

Craig
view

Bowling
Green

Bridgeness

Carriden
Glade

Bridgeness
Lane

Carriden

PHILPINGSTONE

Fountainpark
Cres

Bowling
Green

Grange

GRANGE LOAN

HARBOUR

Kinningars Park

Kinacres Grove

Foredale
Terr

Cuffabouts

Carriden

GRAHAMSDYKE

Grahamsdyke Lane

Grahams
Ave

4 4

G R A H A M S D Y K E

Graham Crescent

Seton
Terr

Bo'ness
Academy

Hadrian Way

DRUM ROAD

CARRIDEN BRAE

Drum
Farm

Academy

hamsdyke

Drumpark Ave

Drumacre Road

Muirend Ct

Carriden Burn

Muirhouses

Glen Ard
View

A993

G R A H A M S D Y K E   R O A D

Acre Road

Football
Field

Playing
Fields

3 3

Bonhard
Ct

Bonhard Way

Hope Cotts

Little
Carriden

Gledhill

Avenue

Miller
Cres

A904

To Linlithgow &
Queensferry

2 2

Redbrae
Cottages

Northbank

Bonhard
Cottages

1 1

G 01 H J 02

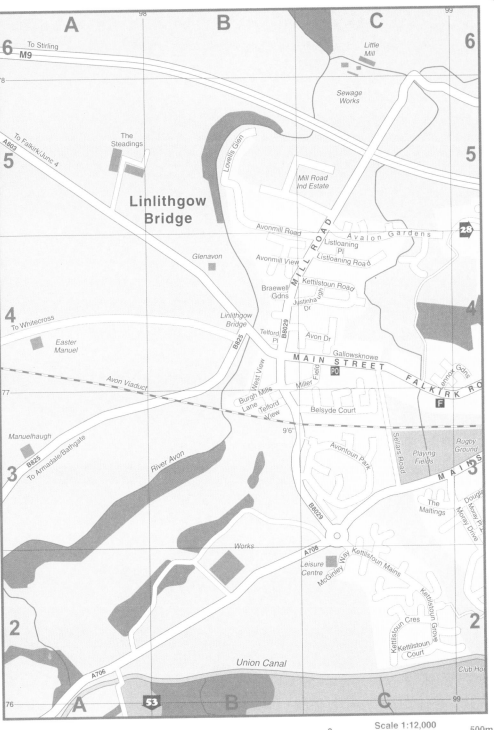

Scale 1:12,000

0   500m

0   500yds

D 6

To Bo'ness
A706

E

F

Parkhead
Small Holdings

B8029

Parkhead

Mount
Michael

Loch
House

5

Linlithgow Loch

Clark Avenue

Parkhead Road

The Rickle

St Ninian's
Avenue

27

Clark Ave

Bow
Butts

Lade
Court

Jock's Hill

Lochmill

Low Port

Mill
Lade

St Ninian's Road

Linlithgow
Palace
(rems of)

Jock's Hill Cres

Longcroft Gardens

Bowling
Green

4

Highfield Crescent

Philip Avenue

A706

St Ninian's Way

Kirkgate

Market
Ln

Liby

1 St Michael's Wynd
2 Dog Well Wynd
3 Brae Court

Highfield Ave

Gdns

St Ninians
Park

The Vennel

The Cross

HIGH ST

Ashley
Court

A803

WEST PORT

HIGH STREET

Whitten Ln

Water
Yett

Tanners
Wynd

Well
Wynd

3

HIGH
Por

PO

1

Station

K ROAD

Linlithgow

A706

Hamilton
Park

St Johns
Ave

New Way

Union Road

Station
Rd

Back Station Rd

Ashley
Hall Gdns

West Port Pl

Royal Terrace

Strawberry Bank

Avon Pl

Canal Ter

Clarendon Crescent

12'9"

ONS ROAD

Preston
Ct

Huntingtower Ct

Victoria
Place

m

Rockville
Grove

Clarendon Rd

Rugby
Ground

Preston Ave

Preston Terrace

Preston Cres

Preston Park

Friars
Loan

Rosemount
Park

Cla
He

3

Cemetery

Park Rd

Friars Brae

Douglas Ave

Merker Terrace

Prestonfield
Park

St Josephs

Priory Road

Burgess
Hill

Rivaldsgreen Crescent

Waldie Ave

Manse Road

Oatlands Park

Moray Pl
Douglas Pl

Stewart Ave
Hamilton Ave

Linlithgow
Academy

Linlithgow

PRESTON ROAD

FRIARS
WAY

Deacons Cl

Laverock
Park

Moray Drive

R A E H E A D

Braehead
Place

Deanburn Park

Riccarton Rd

Carmel

Beechwood

The Glebe

2

Braehead
Pk

Braehead Terrace

DEANBURN ROAD

RICCARTON ROAD

Golf Course Rd

8'6"

Club House

Acredales

Dark Entry

D

E

00

F

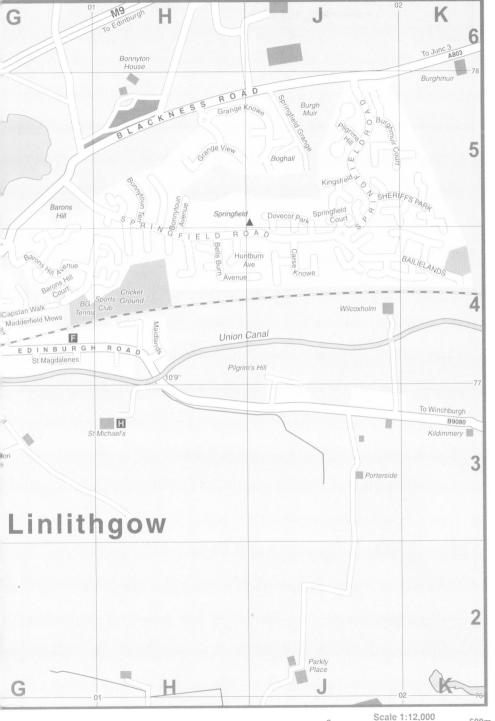

G H J K

01 02

M9
To Edinburgh

6

To Junc 3
A803
Burghmuir
78

Bonnyton
House

BLACKNESS ROAD

Grange Knowe

Springfield Grange

Burgh
Muir

Pilgrims
Hill

Burghmuir Court

SPRINGFIELD ROAD

5

Grange View

Boghall

Kingsfield

SHERIFFS PARK

Barons
Hill

Bonnytoun Terr

Bonnytoun Avenue

Springfield

Dovecot Park

Springfield
Court

S P R I N G F I E L D   R O A D

Bells Burn

Huntburn
Ave

Carse
Knowe

BAILIELANDS

Barons Hill Avenue

Barons Hill
Court

Capstan Walk

Madderfield Mews

BG
Tennis

Sports
Club

Cricket
Ground

Maidlands

Wilcoxholm

4

Union Canal

EDINBURGH ROAD

F

St Magdalenes

10'9"

Pilgrim's Hill

To Winchburgh
B9080

77

Kildimmery

St Michael's

H

Porterside

3

Linlithgow

2

Parkly
Place

G H J K

01 02 76

Scale 1:12,000

0 .... 500m
0 .... 500yds

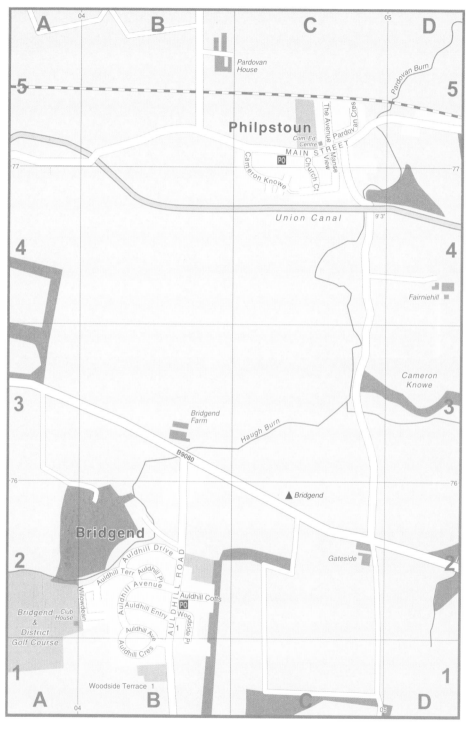

A   B   C   D

5   Pardovan House   Pardovan Burn   5

Philpstoun

The Avenue   Pardovan Cres

Com Ed Centre   MAIN STREET   Manse

PO   Church Ct   View

Cameron Knowe

77   77

Union Canal   9'3"

4   4

Fairniehill

Cameron Knowe

3   Bridgend Farm   3

Haugh Burn

B9080

76   ▲ Bridgend   76

Bridgend   Gateside

Auldhill Drive

Auldhill Terr   Auldhill Pl   AULDHILL ROAD

2   Auldhill Avenue   Auldhill Cotts   2

Willowdean   Auldhill Entry   PO

Bridgend & District Golf Course   Club House   Auldhill Ave   Woodside Pl

Auldhill Cres

1   Woodside Terrace 1   1

A   B   C   D

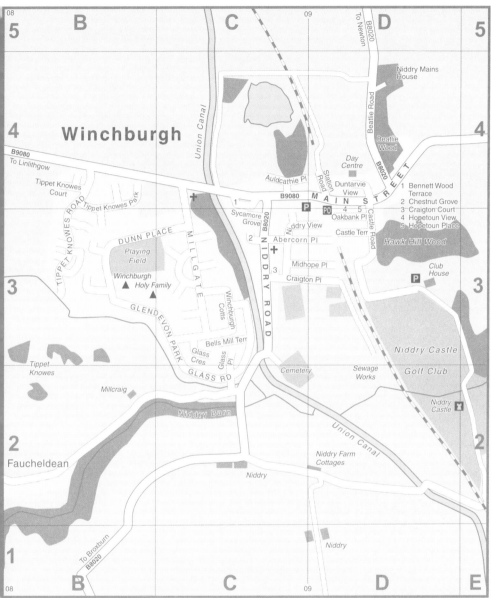

INDEX TO STREET NAMES - WINCHBURGH

Abercorn Pl	C3	Criagton Ct (3)	C3	Hopetoun Pl (5)	D3	Station Rd	D4
Auldcathie Pl	C4	Craigton Pl	C3	Hopetoun Vw (4)	D3	Sycamore Gro	C3
Beatlie Rd	D4	Dunn Pl	B3	Main St	D4	Tippet Knowes Ct	B4
Bell's Mill Terr	C3	Duntarvie Vw	D4	Midhope Pl	C3	Tippet Knowes Pk	B4
Bennet Wood Terr (1)	C4	Glass Cres	C3	Millgate	C3	Tippet Knowes Rd	B3
Castle Rd	D3	Glass Pl	C3	Niddry Rd	C3	Winchburgh Cotts	C3
Castle Terr	D3	Glass Rd	C2	Niddry Vw	C3		
Chestnut Gro (2)	C3	Glendevon Pk	B3	Oakbank Pl	D3		

Scale 1:12,000

0 — 500m
0 — 500yds

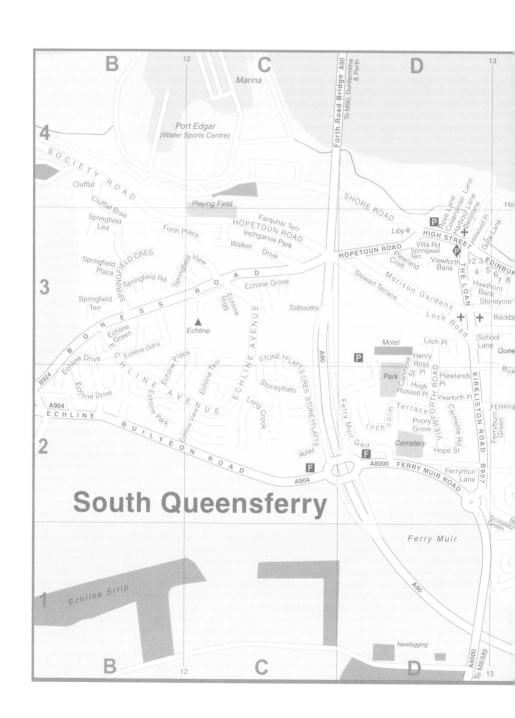

Marina

Port Edgar
(Water Sports Centre)

Forth Road Bridge A90
To M90, Dunfermline & Perth

S O C I E T Y   R O A D

Clufflat

Clufflat Brae

Springfield Lea

Forth Place

Playing Field

Farquhar Terr

HOPETOUN ROAD

Inchgarvie Park

Walker   Drive

SHORE ROAD

Liby

HIGH STREET

Rose Lane
Covenanter Lane
Harbour Lane
Bellslane

Hillwood Pl

Gote Lane

Ha

HOPETOUN ROAD

Villa Rd
Springwell
Terr
Plewland
Croft

Viewforth
Bank

EDINBU

12 3
4 5 6 7 8

THE LOAN

Hawthorn
Bank

Stoneycro

Springfield
Place

SPRINGFIELD CRES

Springfield Rd

Springfield View

Springfield Terr

Echline
Rigg

Echline Grove

Echline

Stewart Terrace

Morison Gardens

Loch Road

Tolbooths

B O N N E S S   R O A D

Echline
Green

Echline Drive

Echline Gdns

Echline Place

Echline Terr

E C H L I N E   A V E N U E

STONEYFLATTS CRES

Stoneyflatts

Motel

Loch Pl

Henry
Ross
Pl

Park

Cranmore
St

Hugh
Russell Pl

Plewlands
Pl

Viewforth Pl

School
Lane

Que

Bu

Backb

B924

A904
E C H L I N E

Echline Drive

Echline Park

Echline View

Long Crook

S. CRES STONEYFLATTS

PARK

Ferry Muir Gait

Terrace

Priory
Grove

Inch colm

Cemetery

Hope St

VIEWFORTH ROAD

Carmelle Rd

KIRKLISTON ROAD

FERRY

Ferryburn
Green

B907

B U I L Y E O N   R O A D

F

A904

F

A8000

FERRY MUIR ROAD

Ferrymuir
Lane

South Queensferry

Ferry Muir

A90

Echline Strip

Newbigging

A8000
To M8/M9

Scotstou
Green

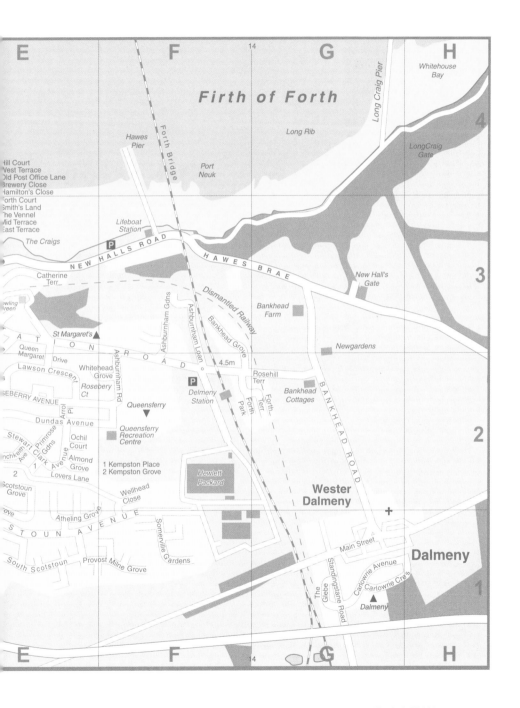

Firth of Forth

E F 14 G H

Whitehouse
Bay

Long Craig Pier

Long Rib

LongCraig
Gate

Hawes
Pier

Forth Bridge

4

Port
Neuk

Hill Court
West Terrace
Old Post Office Lane
Brewery Close
Hamilton's Close
Forth Court
Smith's Land
The Vennel
Mid Terrace
East Terrace

Lifeboat
Station

The Craigs

P

NEW HALLS ROAD

HAWES BRAE

New Hall's
Gate

3

Catherine
Terr

owling
reen

Bankhead
Farm

A T I O N

St Margaret's ▲

Ashburnham Gdns

Ashburnham Loan

Dismantled Railway

Bankhead Grove

Newgardens

Queen
Margaret   Drive

R O A D

4.5m

Rosehill
Terr

BANKHEAD ROAD

Lawson Crescen

Whitehead
Grove

Ashburnham Rd

P

Bankhead
Cottages

EBERY AVENUE

Rosebery
Ct

Delmeny
Station

Forth
Terr

Arrol Pl

Queensferry ▼

Forth
Park

2

Dundas Avenue

Stewart Clark Ave

Primrose Gdns

Ochil
Court

Queensferry
Recreation
Centre

nchkeith
Ave

1   Ave

Almond
Grove

1 Kempston Place
2 Kempston Grove

Scotstoun
Grove

2

Lovers Lane

Hewlett
Packard

**Wester
Dalmeny**

rove

STOUN   AVENUE

Wellhead
Close

Atheling Grove

Somerville Gardens

Somerville Gardens

Main Street

+

Dalmeny

South Scotstoun

Provost Milne Grove

The Glebe

Standingstane Road

Carlowrie Avenue

Carlowrie Cres

▲
Dalmeny

1

E F 14 G H

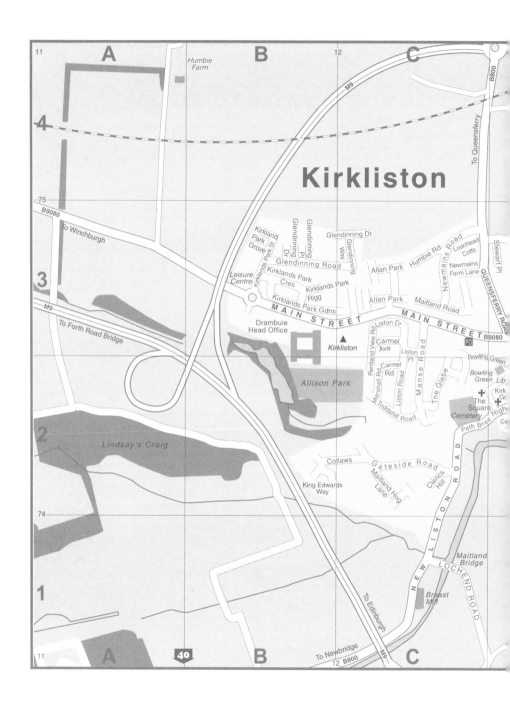

Kirkliston

Humbie Farm

M9

B800

To Queensferry

11

A

B

12

C

4

75

B9080

To Winchburgh

3

M9

To Forth Road Bridge

2

Lindsay's Craig

74

1

11

A

40

B

12

B800

To Newbridge

C

Kirkland Park Grove

Glendinning Dr

Glendinning Pl

Glendinning Way

Glendinning

Loanhead Cotts

Humbie Rd

Newmains Road

Stewart Pl

Glendinning Road

Leisure Centre

Kirklands Park Cres

Allan Park

Newmains Farm Lane

Kirklands Park

Kirklands Park Rigg

Allan Park

Maitland Road

Kirklands Park Gdns

Queensferry Road

MAIN STREET

MAIN STREET

B9080

P0

Drambuie Head Office

▲ Kirkliston

Liston Dr

Carmel Ave

Liston Pl

Pentland View Rd

Carmel Rd

Liston Road

Manse Road

Bowling Green

Bowling Green

Lib

Marshall Rd

Toddshill Road

The Glebe

Kirk Gd

Kirk High

Allison Park

The Square

Cemetery

Path Brae

Cotlaws

Gateside Road

Maitland Hog Lane

Clerics Hill

King Edwards Way

NEW LISTON ROAD

LOCHEND ROAD

Maitland Bridge

To Edinburgh

Breast Mill

M9

INDEX TO STREET NAMES - KIRKLISTON

Allan Pk	C3
Allison Pl	D3
Almondhill Rd	D3
Almondside	D2
Auldgate	D2
Bowling Green Rd	D2
Carmel Ave	C3
Carmel Rd	C2
Clerics Hill	C2
Cobbler's Cl	D2
Cotlaws	C2
Dungeon Pl	D3
Dundas Pl	D3
Gateside Rd	C2
Glebe, The	C2
Glendinning Dr	C3
Glendinning Pl	B3
Glendinning Rd	B3
Glendinning Way	C3
High St	D2
Humbie Rd	C3
King Edwards Way	B2
Kirklands Park Cres	B3
Kirklands Park Gdns	B3
Kirklands Park Gro	B3
Kirklands Park Rigg	B3
Kirklands Park St	B3
Kirkstyle Gdns	D2
Liston Dr	C3
Liston Pl	C3
Liston Rd	C2
Loanhead Cotts	C3
Main St	C3
Maitland Hog La	C2
Maitland Rd	C3
Manse Rd	C2
Marshall Rd	C2
New Liston Rd	C1
Newmains Rd	C3
Newmains Farm La	C3
Path Brae	C2
Pentland View Rd	C2
Queensferry Rd	D3
Square, The	C2
Station Rd	D2
Station Terr	D2
Stewart Pl	D3
Toddshill Rd	C2
Wellflats Rd	D2

Scale 1:12,000

0   500m

0   500yds

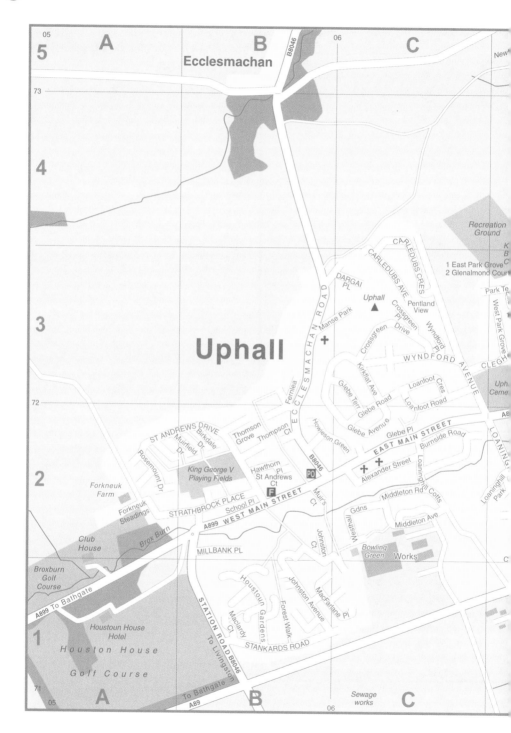

Ecclesmachan

Uphall

Recreation Ground

1 East Park Grove
2 Glenalmond Court

Pentland View

Uphall View

CARLEDUBS CRES
CARLEDUBS AVE
DARGAI PL
Manse Park
Crossgreen Pl
Crossgreen Drive
WYNDFORD AVENUE
Wyndford Pl
Kirkflat Ave
Glebe Terr
Glebe Road
Glebe Avenue
Glebe Pl
Loantoot Cres
Loanfoot Road
EAST MAIN STREET
Burnside Road
Alexander Street
Fernlea
Thomson Grove
Thompson Ct
Howieson Green
Hawthorn Pl
St Andrews Ct
PO
Muirs Ct
Loaninghill Cotts
Middleton Rd Cotts
Middleton Ave
Loaninghill Park
LOANING
ST ANDREWS DRIVE
Birkdale Dr
Muirfield Dr
Rosemount Dr
King George V Playing Fields
School Pl
STRATHBROCK PLACE
A899 WEST MAIN STREET
MILLBANK PL
Johnston Ct
Westhall Gdns
Bowling Green
Works
Forkneuk Farm
Forkneuk Steadings
Club House
Brox Burn
Broxburn Golf Course
A899 To Bathgate
Houstoun House Hotel
Houston House Golf Course
Houstoun Gardens
Maclarty Ct
Forest Walk
Johnston Avenue
MacFarlane Pl
STANKARDS ROAD
STATION ROAD B8046
To Livingston
To Bathgate
A89
Sewage works

West Park Grove
Park Te
Uph. Ceme
CLEGH

B8046
New

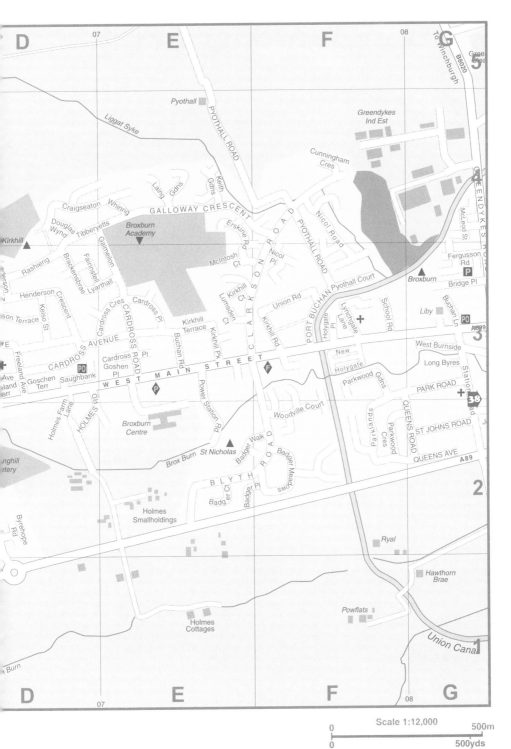

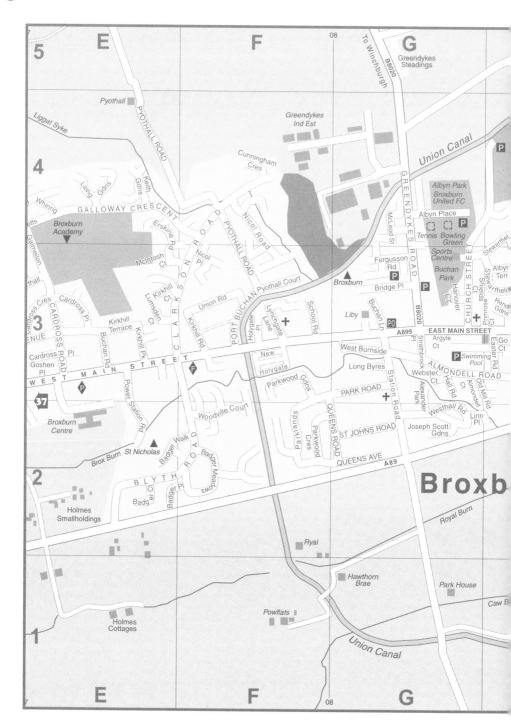

H   09   J   K   10   L

5

73

Albyn
Industrial
Estate

Brocks Way

Clifton View

Youngs Road

Peniel
Place

SIMPSON ROAD

DUNNET WAY

DROVERS ROAD

eation
und

East   Mains

Industrial

WESTERTON ROAD   Estate

4

HILLVIEW AVENUE

Hillview Pl

Freskyn Pl

AITKEN ORR DRIVE

Tartraven Pl

To Edinburgh

A89

CURRAN CRESCENT

Thistle
Business
Park

Liggat Syke Pl

EDINBURGH ROAD

Brox Burn

F

3

uir

EAST MAIN STREET

A899

Newhouses Rd

Hunter Kilpunt
Gdns   View

Kilpunt
Roundabout

Kilpunt
Gdns

A89

Burnside

72

n

Burnvale

Brox Burn

NEWHOUSES ROAD

Kilpunt

2

Newhouses

Motel

To Edinburgh

M8

Learielaw

1

H   To Glasgow   J   K   L

M8   09   3.9m   10   71

Scale 1:12,000

0   500m

0   500yds

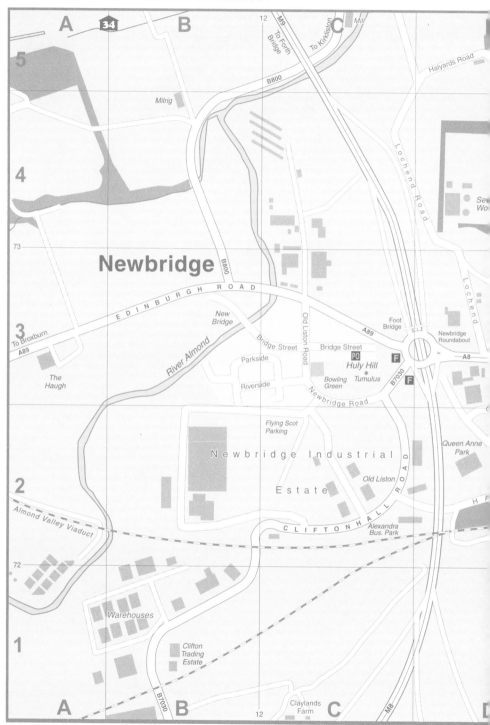

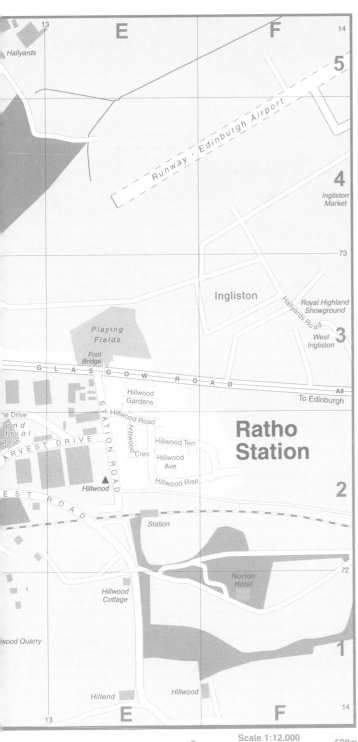

INDEX TO STREET NAMES - NEWBRIDGE & RATHO STATION

Cliftonhall Rd	C2
Edinburgh Rd	B3
Glasgow Rd	E3
Halyards Rd	D5
Halyards Rd	F3
Harvest Dr	D2
Harvest Rd	D2
Hillwood Ave	E2
Hillwood Cres	E2
Hillwood Gdns	E3
Hillwood Rise	E2
Hillwood Rd	E2
Hillwood Terr	E2
Lochend Rd	C4
Newbridge Rd	C3
Old Liston Rd	C3
Parkside	B3
Queen Anne Dr	D2
Riverside	B3
Station Rd	E2

Scale 1:12,000

0   500m

0   500yds

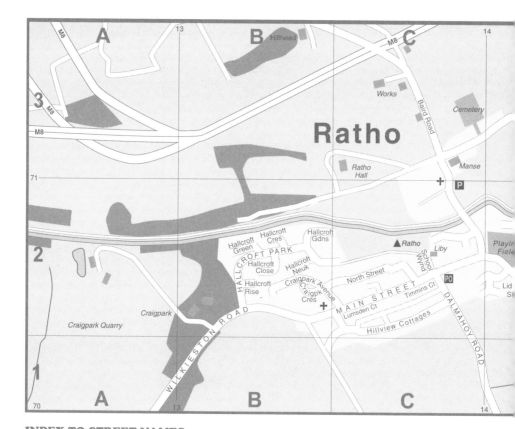

INDEX TO STREET NAMES -
UPHALL & BROXBURN

Aitken Orr Dr	39 H3	Cardross Rd	37 E3	Fergusson Rd	38 G3	Hoban Sq	39 H
Albyn Pl	38 G4	Carledubs Ave	36 C3	Fernlea	36 B3	Holmes Farm La	37 D
Albyn Terr	38 H3	Carledubs Cres	36 C4	Forest Wk	36 B1	Holmes Rd	37 D
Alexander Pk	38 G3	Church St	38 G3	Forkneuk Steading	36 A2	Holygate Pl	38 F
Alexander St	36 C2	Clarkson Rd	37 E3	Freeland Ave	37 D3	Houston Gdns	36 B
Almondell Ct	38 G3	Cleghorn Dr	36 D3	Freeland Terr	37 D3	Howieson Grn	36 B
Almondell Rd	38 G3	Clifton Vw	39 J5	Freskyn Pl	39 J4	Hunter Gdns	39
Argyle Ct	38 G3	Craigengar	36 D2	Galloway Cres	37 E4	Johnston Ave	36 B
Badger Ct	37 E2	Craigseaton	37 D4	Galmeilon	37 E3	Johnston Ct	36 B
Badger Meadows	38 F2	Crossgreen Dr	36 C3	Glebe Ave	36 C2	Joseph Scott Cres	38 G
Badger Pl	37 E2	Crossgreen Pl	36 C3	Glebe Pl	36 C2	Keith Gdns	37 E
Badger Walk	37 E2	Cunningham Cres	38 F4	Glebe Rd	36 C2	Kelso St	37 D
Birkdale Dr	36 B2	Curran Cres	39 H3	Glebe Terr	36 C3	Kilpunt Gdns	39
Blairmuir Terr	38 H3	Dargai Pl	36 C3	Glenalmond Ct (2)	36 D3	Kilpunt Vw	39
Blyth Rd	37 E2	Douglas Wynd	37 D4	Gordon Ct	38 H3	Kirkflat Ave	36 C
Brackensbrae	37 D3	Drovers Rd	39 J4	Goschen Pl	37 E3	Kirkhill Ct	37 E
Bridge Pl	38 G3	Dunn St	36 D3	Goschen Terr	37 D3	Kirkhill Pk	37 E
Brocks Way	39 J5	Dunnet Way	39 J4	Grange Rd	38 H2	Kirkhill Rd	38 F
Buchan La	38 G3	Easter Rd	38 H3	Greendykes Rd	38 G4	Kirkhill Terr	37 E
Buchan Rd	37 E3	East Main St	36 C2	Hall Rd	38 G3	Laing Gdns	37 E
Burn Vale	39 J2	East Main St	38 G3	Hanover Ct	38 G3	Liggat Pl	39 H
Burnside Rd	36 C2	East Park Gro (1)	36 D3	Hawthorn Pl	36 B2	Liggat Syke Pl	39
Byrehope Rd	37 D2	Ecclesmachan Rd	36 B3	Henderson Cres	37 D3	Linn Pl	38 C
Cardross Ave	37 D3	Ellis Pl	36 D3	Henderson Pl	37 D3	Loanfoot Cres	36 C
Cardross Cres	37 E3	Erskine Rd	37 E4	Hillview Ave	39 H4	Loanfoot Rd	36 C
Cardross Pl	37 E3	Fairnsfell	37 D3	Hillview Pl	39 H3	Loaning Hill Cotts	36 C

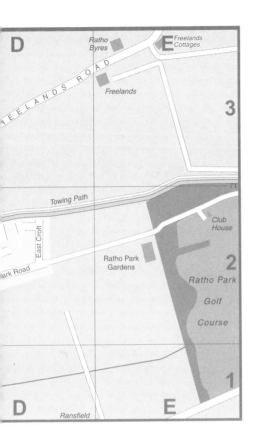

INDEX TO STREET NAMES - RATHO

Craigpark Ave	B2
Craigpark Cres	B2
Dalmahoy Rd	C2
East Croft	D2
Freelands Rd	D3
Hallcroft Cl	B2
Hallcroft Cres	B2
Hallcroft Gdns	B2
Hallcroft Grn	B2
Hallcroft Neuk	B2
Hallcroft Pk	B2
Hallcroft Rise	B2
Hillview Cotts	C2
Lidgate Shot	D2
Lumsden Ct	C2
Main St	C2
North St	C2
Ratho Park Rd	D2
School Wynd	C2
Timmins Ct	C2
West Croft	D2
Wilkieston Rd	A1

Scale 1:12,000

0   500m
0   500yds

Loaning Hill Pk	36 C2	Park Rd	38 G3	Stewartfield Cres	38 H3
Loaning Hill Rd	36 D2	Park Terr	36 D3	Stewartfield Rd	38 H3
Long Byres	38 G3	Parkview	36 D3	Strathbrock Pl	36 B2
Lumsden Ct	37 E3	Parkwood Cres	38 F2	Strathbrock Pl	38 G3
Lyarthall	37 D3	Parkwood Gdns	38 F3	Tartraven Pl	39 J3
Lynchgate La	38 F3	Patersons Ct	39 H3	Thomson Ct	36 B2
MacFarlane Pl	36 B1	Pentland Vw	36 C3	Thomson Gro	36 B2
Maclardy Ct	36 B1	Port Buchan	38 F3	Timmeryetts	37 D4
McCann Ave	36 D3	Primrose Ct	38 H3	Union Rd	38 F3
McIntosh Ct	37 E3	Pyothall Ct	38 F3	Webster Ct	38 G3
McLeod St	38 G4	Pyothall Rd	38 F4	West Burnside	38 G3
Manse Pk	36 B3	Queens Ave	38 G2	Westerton Rd	39 K3
Melbourne Rd	39 H3	Queens Rd	38 G2	Westhall Gdns	36 C2
Middleton Ave	36 C2	Rashierig	37 D3	Westhall Rd	38 G2
Middleton Rd	36 C2	Rendall Gdns	38 H3	West Main St	36 B2
Millbank Pl	36 B2	Rosemount Dr	36 A2	West Main St	37 E3
Muirfield Dr	36 B2	St Andrews Dr	36 A2	West Park Gro	36 D3
Muirs Ct	36 B2	St John's Rd	38 G2	Whinrig	37 E4
New Holygate	38 F3	Saughbank	37 D3	Wilson Terr	37 D3
Newhouses Rd	39 J2	School Pl	36 B2	Woodville Ct	38 F2
Nicol Pl	38 F3	School Rd	38 F3	Wyndford Ave	36 C3
Nicol Rd	38 F4	Shiels Ct	38 G3	Wyndford Pl	36 C3
Old Mill Rd	38 G3	Simpson Rd	39 K4	Youngs Rd	39 J4
Old Town	38 H3	Stankards Rd	36 B1		
Parklands	38 F2	Station Rd	36 B1		
Park Ct	36 D3	Station Rd	38 G3		

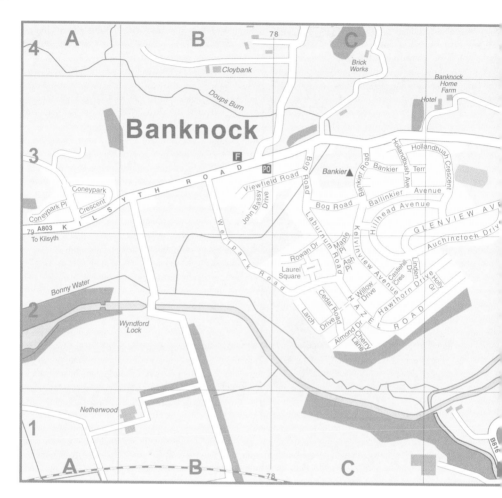

INDEX TO STREET NAMES - BANKNOCK

Almond Dr	C2	Cedar Rd	C2	Hawthorn Dr	
Anderson Terr	F3	Cherry Lane	C2	Hazel Rd	
Ash Pl	C2	Coneypark Cres	A3	Hillhead Ave	
Auchincloch Dr	D2	Coneypark Pl	A3	Hollandbush Ave	
Ballinker Ave	C3	Cumbernauld Rd	E3	Hollandbush Cres	
Bankier Rd	C3	Doctor's Brae	F4	Holly Gro	
Bankier Terr	C3	Dundas Cotts	E2	James St	
Bog Rd	C3	Garngrew Rd	D3	John St	
Castlehill Cres	C2	Glasgow Rd	E3	John Bassey Dr	
Castleview Terr	E3	Glenview Ave	D3	Kelvinview Ave	

Scale 1:12,000

0   500m

0   500yds

Kerr Cres	E3	Rowan Dr	C2
Kilsyth Rd	A3	Station Rd	F4
Laburnum Rd	C3	Thorndale Gdns	F2
Larch Dr	C2	Viewfield Rd	B3
Laurel Sq	C2	Wellpark Cotts	C2
Linden Dr	C2	Wellpark Rd	B3
McVean Pl	F4	Willow Dr	C2
Maple Pl	C2		
Margaret Ave	E3		
Mayfield Dr	F3		

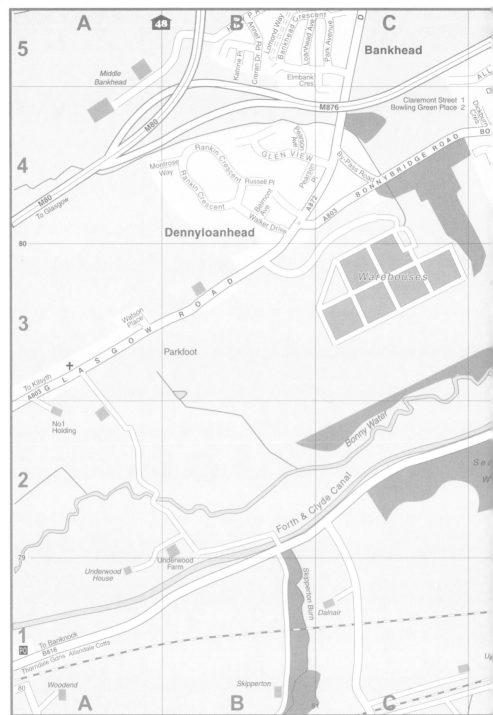

Middle Bankhead

Bankhead

48

GLEN VIEW

M80

M80
To Glasgow

Montrose Way

Rankin Crescent

Rankin Crescent

Russell Pl

Belmont Ave

Walker Drive

Pearson Ave

Pearson Pl

Dennyloanhead

Katrine Pl

Creran Dr

Annel Rd

Lomond Way

Bankhead Crescent

Loanhead Ave

Park Avenue

Elmbank Cres

M876

By-Pass Road

BONNYBRIDGE ROAD

A872

A803

Claremont Street 1
Bowling Green Place 2

Dickburn Cres

Warehouses

Watson Place

GLASGOW ROAD

Parkfoot

To Kilsyth
A803

No1 Holding

Bonny Water

Forth & Clyde Canal

Skipperton Burn

Underwood Farm

Underwood House

Dalnair

PO

To Banknock
B816

Thorndale Gdns   Ailandale Cotts

Woodend

Skipperton

80

79

80

81

A

B

C

D

5

4

3

2

1

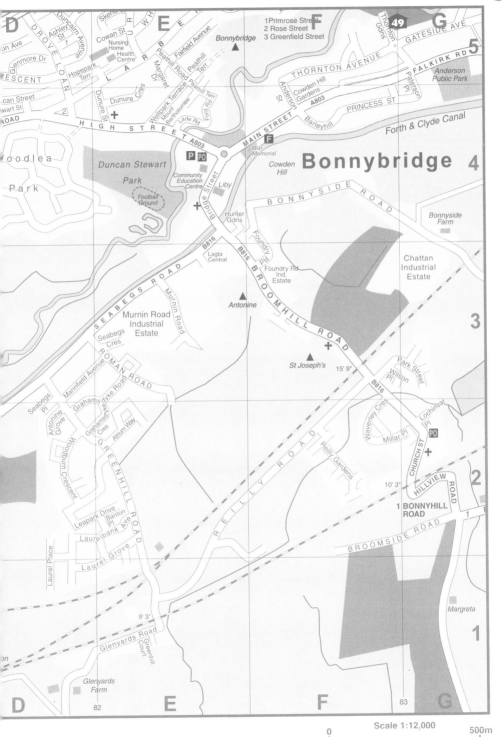

Bonnybridge

1 Primrose Street
2 Rose Street
3 Greenfield Street

Scale 1:12,000

0 — 500m
0 — 500yds

Stoneywood

1 St Johns Gate
2 St Johns Grove
3 Overton Terrace
4 Stoneywood Park

1 Langhill Place
2 Dundaff Court
3 Randolph Gardens
4 Garvald Lane

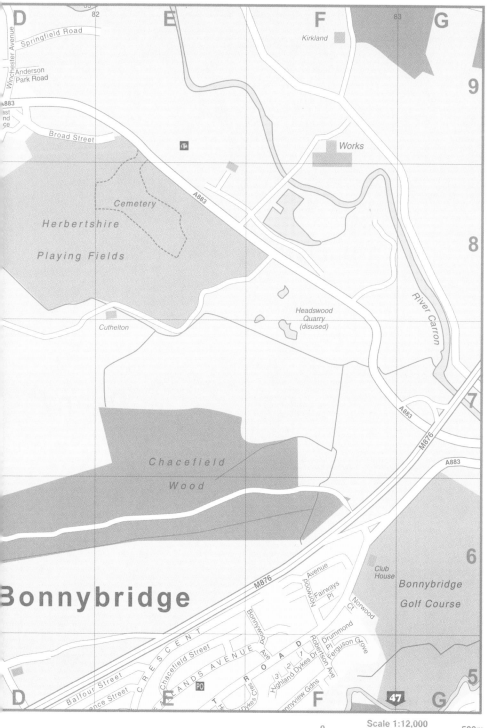

D 82 E F Kirkland 83 G

9

Winchester Avenue
Springfield Road

Anderson
Park Road

A883
ast
nd
ce

Broad Street

Works

Cemetery

Herbertshire

Playing Fields

8

A883

Cuthelton

Headswood
Quarry
(disused)

River Carron

Chacefield

Wood

7

A883

M876

A883

Club
House

Bonnybridge

Golf Course

6

Bonnybridge

M876

Avenue

Norwood

Fairways
Pl

Norwood
Ct

C R E S C E N T

Bonnywood Ave

Drummond
Pl

Robertson Ave

Ferguson Grove

Balfour Street

ence Street

Chacefield Street

PO

L A N D S   A V E N U E

Dykes Cres

3

2

Highland Dykes

onnyview Gdns

R O A D

47

5

D E F G

Scale 1:12,000

0 —————————————— 500m
0 —————————————— 500yds

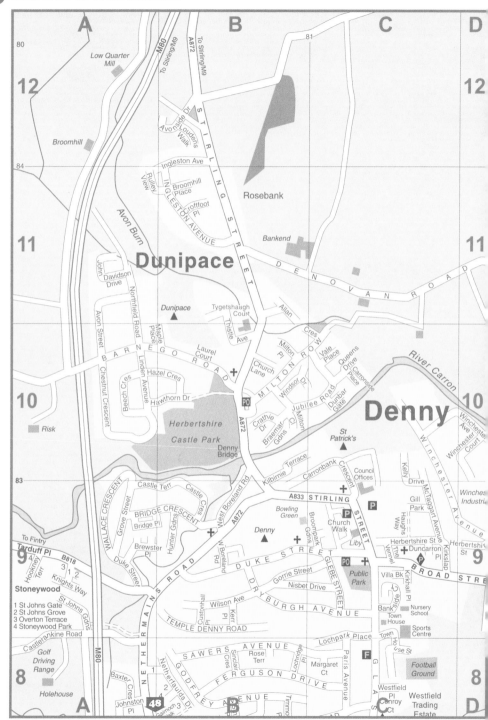

INDEX TO STREET NAMES - WESTFIELD

Lomond Vw	A1
Main St	A2
Millburn Rd	A2
Park Vw	A1
Strathavon Terr	A2
Strathlogie	A2

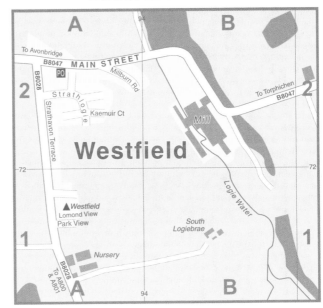

INDEX TO STREET NAMES -AVONBRIDGE

Avon Terr	B2
Blackstone Rd	B2
Bridgend Rd	B2
Bridgehill	B2
Craigbank Rd	B1
Falkirk Rd	A3
Hareburn Ave	B1
Linmill Rd	B1
Main St	B2
Slamannan Rd	A1

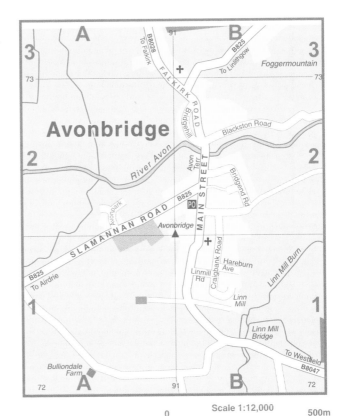

Scale 1:12,000

0   500m

0   500yds

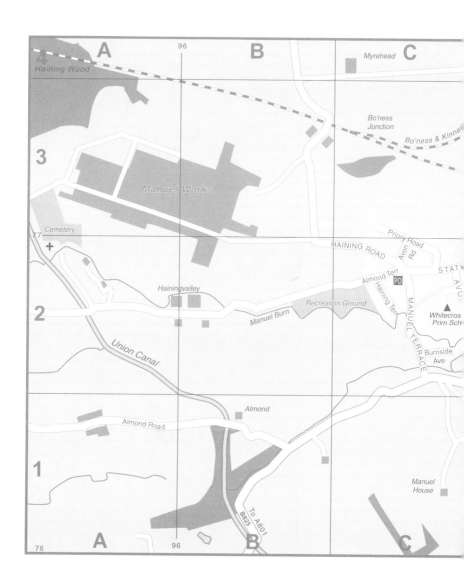

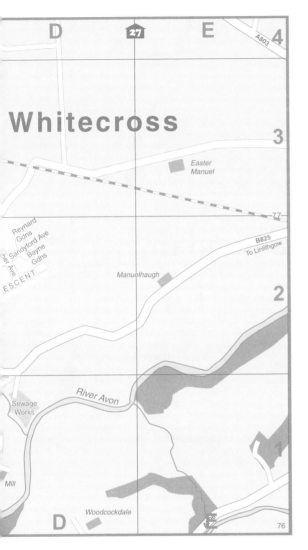

Whitecross

Easter Manuel

Manuelhaugh

Reynard Gdns

Sandyford Ave

Bayne Gdns

Ave

ESCENT

B825
To Linlithgow

River Avon

Sewage Works

Mill

Woodcockdale

D

27

A803

Scale 1:12,000

0   500m
0   500yds

INDEX TO STREET NAMES - WHITECROSS

Alma Cotts	D3
Almond Rd	A1
Almond Terr	C2
Avon Rd	C2
Avontoun Cres	C2
Bayne Gdns	D2
Burnside Gdns	C2
Carriber Ave	D2
Cockburn Cres	D2
Haining Rd	C2
Haining Terr	C2
McLaren Ave	C2
Priory Rd	C3
Reynard Gdns	D2
Sandyford Ave	D2
Station Rd	C2

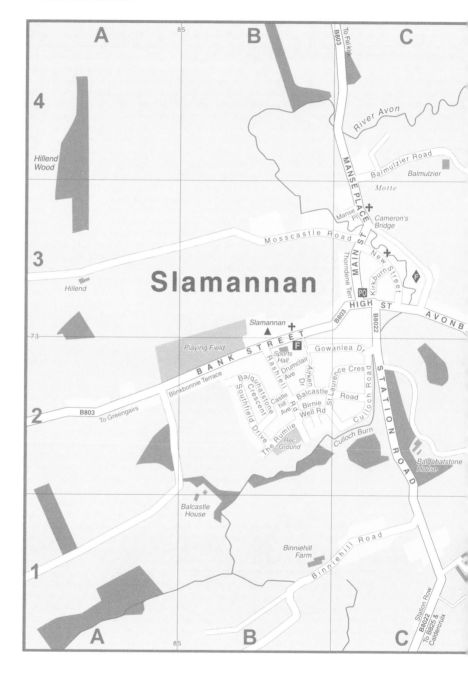

Slamannan

Wester
Loanrigg

Hillhead

ROAD

Peatrigend

Crossburr

B8022
To B825

Wester
Arnloss

stone

INDEX TO STREET NAMES - SLAMANNAN

Aitken Dr	B2
Avonbridge Rd	C3
Balcastle Rd	B2
Balmulzier Rd	C4
Balquhatstone Cres	B2
Bank St	B2
Birniewell Rd	B2
Blinkbonnie Terr	A2
Castlehill Ave	B2
Culloch Rd	C2
Drumclair Ave	B2
Gowanlea Dr	B2
High St	C3
Kirkburn	C3
Main St	C3
Manse Pl	C4
Mosscastle Rd	B3
New St	C3
Rashiehill Rd	B2
Rumlie, The	B2
St Laurence Cres	B2
Southfield Dr	B2
Station Rd	C2
Thorndene Terr	C3

Scale 1:12,000

0   500m

0   500yds

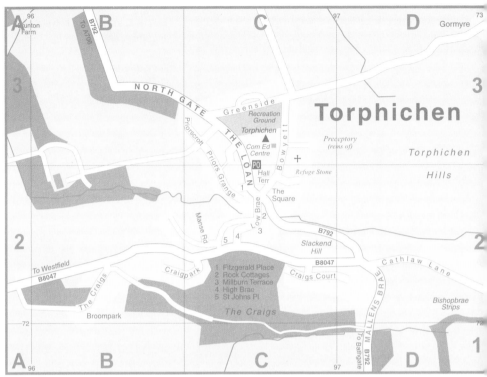

INDEX TO STREET NAMES - TORPHICHEN

Bowyett	C3	Fitzgerald Pl (1)	C2	Mallens Brae	D1	Rock Cotts (2)	C
Broompark	B2	Greenside	C3	Manse Rd	C2	St Johns Pl (5)	C
Cathlaw La	D2	High Brae (4)	C2	Millburn Terr (3)	C2	Square, The	C
Craigpark	B2	Loan, The	C3	North Gate	B3		
Craigs, The	B2	Low Brae	C2	Priorscroft	C3		
Craigs Ct	C2			Priors Grange	C3		

INDEX TO STREET NAMES - SHIELDHILL

Anderson Cres	B4	Easton Dr	B5	Ledi Pl	C5	Pirleyhill Dr	B
Belmont Ave	C5	Elm Dr	A4	Main St	B4	Rannoch Pl	C
Braes Vw	B5	Gardrum Gdns	B5	Mavisbank Ave	A4	Rosemount Gdns	B
Braeside	B4	Greencraig Ave	A4	Muirpark Dr	B4	Vorlich Dr	C
Crimond Pl	C5	Greenmount Dr	A4	Ochil Vw	B5	Wallace Vw	B
Cross Brae	B4	Heather Ave	A4	Parkend Cres	A4		
Crosshall Pl	B4	Herdshill Ave	B4	Paterson Dr	A4		
Cruickshank Dr	B4	High View Gro	B4	Patrick Dr	C5		

Scale 1:12,000

0   500m

0   500yds

F G 63 H J

WALLACESTONE BRAE

Comyn Drive

Balmoral Gardens

Arneil Pl

Mountjoy Cotts

Comely Park

Craigs

SO

SUNNYSIDE ROAD

Sunnyside Cotts

Drive

Park

P

+

5

Wallacelea

Bellvue

Goodman C

Harlington Place

ABERCAIRN

Greenwells

Hamilton Cres

Mac

ROAD

Gardrum Burn

Burnside

4

Bel as Grove

Ing Pl

andrigg

60

Manuel Burn

3

Glenhead

2

Works

Craigend

F G H J 1

92 93

Scale 1:12,000

0 500m

0 500yds

F
G
64
H Balmoral Gardens
J

Keys

LACESTONE BRAE

Comyn Drive

Arneil Pl

Sunnyside Cotts

SUNNYSIDE ROAD

Mountjoy Cotts

Comely Park

SOUT

Craigs Terr

5

Park

P

Wallacelea

Bellvue

Goodman Pl

Harlington Place

Carr

ABERCAIRNE

Hamilton Cres

Greenwells

MacAr

Gardrum Burn

Burnside

C A

Bethesda Grove

4

Ingrar Plac

59

drigg

Manuel Burn

3

Glenhead

2

Works

Craigend

1

F
92
G
H
93
J

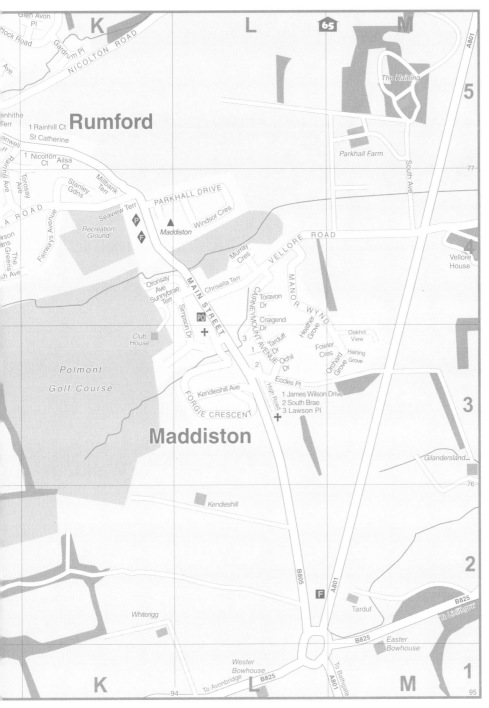

Glen Avon Pl
tock Road
Gardrum Pl
NICOLTON ROAD
Ave

65

The Haining

M

A801

5

enhithe
Terr
1 Rainhill Ct **Rumford**
St Catherine
enwell
1 Nicolton Ailsa
Ct Ct
Rainhill Ave
Torosay Ave
Stanley Gdns
Millbank Terr
PARKHALL DRIVE
Windsor Cres

Parkhall Farm

South Ave

77

A ROAD
Seaview Terr
P
Maddiston
F
Recreation
Ground
Fairways Avenue
son
ns Greens
h Ave
The
Greens

Murray
Cres
VELLORE ROAD

Vellore
House

4

Oronsay
Ave
Sunnybrae
Terr
Chrisella Terr
MAIN STREET
Simpson Dr
PO

MANOR WYND

Toravon
Dr
Craigend
Dr
CAIRNEYMOUNT AVENUE
Tarduff
Dr
3 1 Ochil
Dr
2
Eccles Pl

Heather Grove
Fowler
Cres
Orchard Grove
Oakhill
View
Haining
Grove

Club
House

Polmont
Golf Course

Kendieshill Ave
FORGIE CRESCENT

High Road
1 James Wilson Drive
2 South Brae
3 Lawson Pl

Gilandersland

3

76

Maddiston

Kendieshill

2

B805

A801

F

Tarduf

B825
B825
To Linlithgow

Whiterigg

B825
Easter
Bowhouse

Wester
Bowhouse
To Avonbridge
B825
To Bathgate
A801

K
94
L
M
1
95

Scale 1:12,000

0 ———— 500m
0 ———— 500yds

C 66 D E

Redding House

OVERTON CRES

7

Redding Ind Est

REDDING

6 Union Canal

Business Park

Wesley Pl

Forth

6 **Reddingmuirhead** +

Wester Newlands

Nobel View

SHIELDHILL ROAD

Epworth

Fairhaven Terr

Easter Pirleyhill

Middlerig

B810

Reddingrig Muir

er Burn

5 Belmont Ave BELMONT AVENUE

Patrick Dr

Crimond Pl

Crimond Pl

DRIVE

Ledi Pl

n Gdns

Vorlich Dr

ES VIEW

Rannoch Pl

Wallacestone

nderson Cres

B810

Easter Shieldhill

Polmont Burn

B8028

4

Redding Muir

Whitesiderig Muir

The Craigs

Sewage works

Rosemead Terr

3 C 58 + D E

Church Road

F Meadowbank St G School Vi 67 H ROAD Netherfield Road J

Waverley Park

St Margaret's

Playing Fields

Polmont Sports Centre

Meadowbank

REDDING ROAD

Grange Pl

Polmont Junction

Archibald Russel Court

Polmont Bowling Club

Blairs Cotts

Polmont Station

E R S

7

Canal Walk

UNION PLACE

Victoria Pl Brookside

Pretoria Pl

STATION

H. M.

Playing Fields

Cricket Pl

Harlow Ave

RANDOLPH CRESCENT

Whitesideloan

Glen

Young Offenders

Scottish Prison Service College

Douglas Avenue

Woodside Gdns

PO

Institution

Blairlodge Avenue

The Orchard

Bruce Gdns

MAIN STREET B810

Park View

Inglis Pl

NEWLANDS ROAD B810

REDDING ROAD B805

Holmlea Ave

The Grange

6

Braes

Maranatha Cres

Polwarth Avenue

Kennard Rd

Redding Road

Wallace Cres

Craiglaw Terr

Crossgatehead Rd

Charlotte St

MADDISTON ROAD

Laurie Park

QUARRY BRAE

eside ace

Richmond Dr

Polmont Burn

Briarbrae

Park Terr

Park Gdns

Park Dr

Brightons

WAGGON ROAD

Forthview Gdns

Hillview Rd

Willowbrae

Braemar Gdns

PARK AVENUE

Playing Fields

Wallacestone

Balmoral Gardens

64

Comyn Drive

Arneil Pl

Sunnyside Cotts

Mounjoy Cotts

Comely Park

F

5

WALLACESTONE BRAE

SUNNYSIDE ROAD

Wallacelea

Bellvue

Drive

Park

Harlington Place

Goodman Ca

Goodman Pl

P

ABERCAIRN

ROAD

Gardrum Burn

Greenwells

Hamilton Cres

Mac

4

Burnside

Bethus Grove

Ingr Pl

ndrigg

F G 59 H Manuel Burn J 3

GILSTON CRESCENT

TOLSTA CRESCENT

K

Rodel Drive

Taransay Pl

Lewis Rd

Tarbert Pl

GILSTON CRESCENT

Miller Park

ILL

PORTREE CRESCENT

L

Colduie Circle

Dunvegan Place

Forfar Pl

Ardmore Dr

Taymouth Rd

GILSTON CRESCENT

MONTROSE ROAD

Alyth Dr

Forest View

Glamis Gdns

Brechin Dr

69

Gilston

Polmont

M

7

Gilston Burn

78

Union Canal

Battock

Nicolton

Ave

elea Dr

verdale Rd

AD

Greenwells Dr

Glen Avon Pl

Battock Road

on Ave

Gardrum Pl

NICOLTON ROAD

Bethankie Bridge

North Ave

The Haining

A801

6

5

eenhithe Terr

eenwell Terr

Rumford

1 Rainhill Ct

St Catherine

1 Nicolton Ct

Ailsa Ct

Rainhill Ave

Torrosay Ave

Stanley Gdns

Millbank Terr

Parkhall Farm

South Ave

77

IA ROAD

erson dns

The Greens

ith Ave

Fairways Avenue

Seaview Terr

Recreation Ground

P

F

Maddiston

PARKHALL DRIVE

Windsor Cres

VELLORE ROAD

Vello House

4

Oronsay Ave

Sunnybrae Terr

MAIN STREET

Chrisella Terr

Murray Cres

MANOR

Toravon Dr

Craigend Dr

CHIMNEYMOUNT AVENUE

Tarduff Dr

Ochil Dr

WYND

Heather Grove

Haining Grove

Orchard Grove

Oakhill View

Fowler Cres

PO

Club House

+

Simpson Dr

3

1

2

Eccles Pl

61

L

M

Polmont Golf Course

K

ill Ave

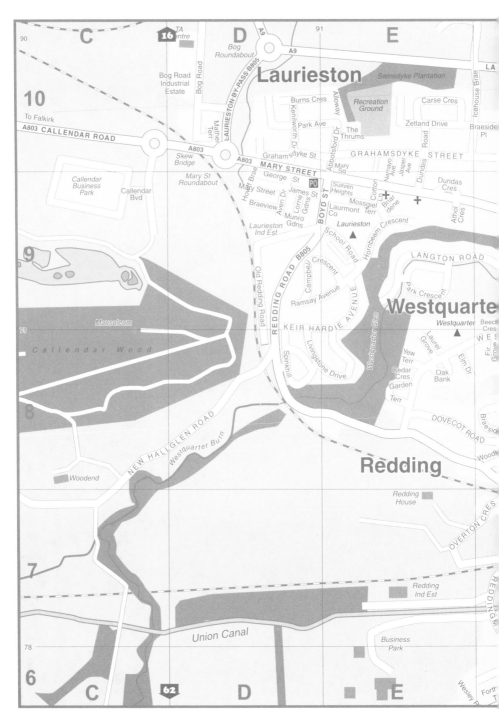

C 90

D

E

91

TA Centre
16

Bog Roundabout
A9

Laurieston

Swinedyke Plantation

LA

Bog Road Industrial Estate

Bog Road

Burns Cres

Alloway

Kenilworth Dr

Recreation Ground

Carse Cres

Icehouse Brae

10

To Falkirk

A803 CALLENDAR ROAD

Mather Terr

Park Ave

The Thrums

Zetland Drive

Braeside Pl

LAURIESTON-BY-PASS-B805

A803

Skew Bridge

Mary St Roundabout

A803

Grahamsdyke St

MARY STREET

George St

PO

GRAHAMSDYKE STREET

Mary Sq

Abbotsford Dr

Road

Namayo Ave

Jasper Ave

Dundas St

Dundas Cres

Callendar Business Park

Callendar Bvd

Mary Street

Holly Brae

James St

Lome Gdns

Aven Dr

Sulven Heights

Cotton

Mossgiel Co

Briar dene

Athol Cres

Braeview

Munro Gdns

Laurmont Terr

Laurieston Ind Est

BOYD ST

School Road

Laurieston ▲

Hornbeam Crescent

9

Campbell Crescent

LANGTON ROAD

Park Crescent

REDDING ROAD B805

Ramsay Avenue

Westquarter Glen

Westquarte

Mausoleum

Old Redding Road

KEIR HARDIE AVENUE

Westquarter ▲

Beech Cres

WE S

Callendar Wood

79

Livingstone Drive

Laurel Grove

Yew Terr

Elm Dr

Fir Grove

Spinkhill

Cedar Cres

Oak Bank

Garden Terr

DOVECOT ROAD

Braesio

8

NEW HALLGLEN ROAD

Westquarter Burn

Redding

Woodend

Redding House

Woodv

OVERTON CRES

7

Redding Ind Est

REDDING R

6 78

Union Canal

Business Park

Wesley P

Forth T

C

62

D

E

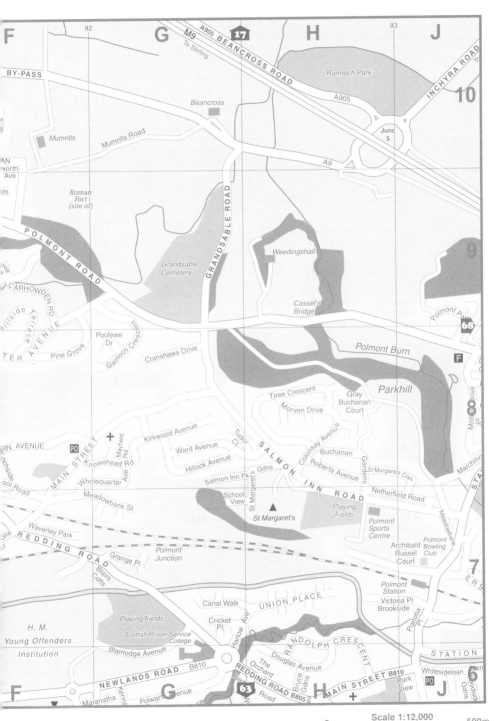

F 92 G **M9** **A905 BEANCROSS ROAD** 17 H 93 J

To Stirling

BY-PASS

Rannoch Park

Beancross

A905

INCHYRA ROAD

To

10

Mumrills

Mumrills Road

Junc 5

A9

AN
worth
Ave

es

Roman
Fort
(site of)

GRANDSABLE ROAD

POLMONT ROAD

Weedingshall

ve

CARHOWDEN RD

Grandsable
Cemetery

Cassel's
Bridge

9

Polmont Park

68

llside Terrace

AVENUE

Poolewe
Dr

Pine Grove

Gairloch Crescent

Cranshaws Drive

Polmont Burn

F

TER

Tiree Crescent

Gray
Buchanan
Court

Parkhill

Morven Drive

Millside Drive

Kirkwood Avenue

Tudor
Ct

Colonsay Avenue

S A L M O N

Buchanan

Gardens

St Margarets Cres

Marchm

RN AVENUE

PO

Knowehead Rd

Mayfield
Rd

Ward Avenue

Roberts Avenue

I N N

STA

chside
ool Road

MAIN STREET

Wholequarter

Ave

Hillock Avenue

Salmon Inn Pk

St Margarets Gdns

R O A D

Netherfield Road

Meadowbank

Meadowbank St

School
View

St Margarets Ave

St Margaret's

Playing
Fields

Polmont
Sports
Centre

Polmont
Bowling
Club

7

Waverley Park

R E D D I N G R O A D

Grange Pl

Polmont
Junction

Archibald
Russel
Court

E R S

Blairs
Cotts

Canal Walk

Harlow Ave

U N I O N P L A C E

Polmont
Station

Victoria Pl
Brookside

Prettotia
Pl

H. M.
Young Offenders

Institution

Playing Fields

Scottish Prison Service
College

Cricket
Pl

The
Orchard

R A N D O L P H C R E S C E N T

Douglas Avenue

STATION

Blairlodge Avenue

N E W L A N D S R O A D B810

63

Maranatha

Kenn

Polwarth Avenue

G

Road

REDDING ROAD B805

Bruce
Gdns

H

MAIN STREET B810

J

Park
View

PO

Whitesideloan

en
oodside
Gdns

F

Scale 1:12,000

0 _____ 500m

0 _____ 500yds

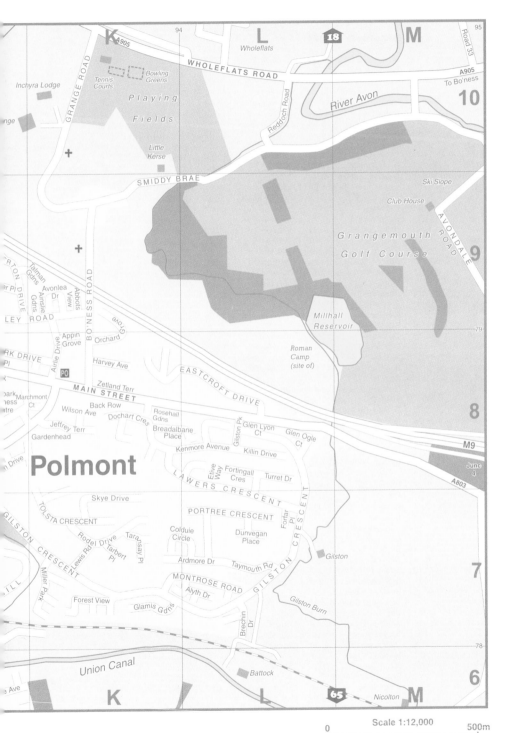

K A905

94

L

Wholeflats

18

M

95

Road 33

WHOLEFLATS ROAD

A905
To Bo'ness

Inchyra Lodge

GRANGE ROAD

Tennis
Courts

Bowling
Greens

P l a y i n g

F i e l d s

Little
Kerse

SMIDDY BRAE

Reddoch Road

River Avon

10

nge

Ski Slope

Club House

AVONDALE ROAD

G r a n g e m o u t h

G o l f   C o u r s e

9

RTON DRIVE

er Pl

LEY ROAD

Talman
Gdns

Avonlea
Dr

Ainslie
Gdns

Abbots View

BO'NESS ROAD

Grove

Appin
Grove

Airlie Drive

Orchard

PO

Harvey Ave

Zetland Terr

MAIN STREET

Millhall
Reservoir

79

Roman
Camp
(site of)

RK DRIVE

Pl

EASTCROFT DRIVE

8

M9

park
ness
tre

Marchmont
Ct

Back Row

Wilson Ave

Jeffrey Terr

Gardenhead

Dochart Cres

Rosehall
Gdns

Breadalbane
Place

Gilston Pk

Glen Lyon
Ct

Glen Ogle
Ct

Kenmore Avenue

Killin Drive

n Drive

Polmont

LAWERS CRESCENT

Etive
Way

Fortingall
Cres

Turret Dr

Junc
4

A803

Skye Drive

PORTREE CRESCENT

Forfar Pl

CRESCENT

GILSTON CRESCENT

TOLSTA CRESCENT

Rodel Drive

Lewis Rd

Tarbert Pl

Taransay Pl

Colduie
Circle

Dunvegan
Place

Gilston

7

Ardmore Dr

Taymouth Rd

MONTROSE ROAD

Alyth Dr

Miller Park

ILL

Forest View

Glamis Gdns

Brechin Dr

Gilston Burn

78

Union Canal

Battock

e Ave

K

L

65

Nicolton

M

6

Scale 1:12,000

0 ———————— 500m

0 ———————— 500yds

70 · INDEX TO STREETS - FALKIRK

Abbots Ct	11 K7	Bank St	10 H5
Abbots Moss Dr	5 E1	Bankside	10 J7
Abbots Rd	11 K7	Bantaskine Dr	5 F4
Abbots Rd	15 K9	Bantaskine Gdns	5 E4
Abbotsford Gdns	14 H9	Bantaskine Rd	5 F4
Abbotsford St	10 H8	Bantaskine St	5 E4
Abercrombie St	9 E6	Barkin Ct (2)	6 H2
Acorn Cres	13 D9	Barnton La (10)	6 H4
Adam Cres	13 F10	Barra Pl	14 G12
Adam Grossert Ct (3)	13 E10	Barrie Rd	13 F11
Adam St	11 K6	Baxter's Wynd	6 H4
Adams Lo	14 G9	Bean Row	6 H4
Affric Dr	14 J9	Beaufort Dr	14 G11
Airthrey Dr	13 F12	Beauly Ct	7 J1
Aitchison Dr	12 B11	Beaumont Dr	14 G10
Aitken Gdns	9 E6	Beech Cres	8 C8
Aitken Rd	9 D6	Begg Ave	5 E4
Aitken Terr	9 D6	Bell's Wynd	6 H4
Akarit Rd	13 E11	Bellevue St	10 J5
Albert Rd	6 G3	Bellsdyke Rd	13 D12
Alexander Ave	11 L5	Bellsmeadow Rd	11 J5
Allan Barr Ct	6 H1	Belmont St	6 J4
Allanbank Rd	12 C10	Belmont Tower	7 J4
Alloa Rd	14 G11	Binnie Pl	15 M10
Alloway Wynd	12 C12	Birnam Ct	15 J9
Alloa Rd	13 F12	Birnam Pl	11 J5
Alma Bank	10 H6	Blackmill Cres	14 H11
Alma La	10 H6	Blair Terr	14 G12
Alma St	10 H6	Blairdenon Cres	5 F3
Alma Terr	10 H6	Bleachfield	10 G6
Almond Ct	11 L7	Blenheim Pl	13 E13
Almond Rd	11 L7	Blinkbonny Rd	5 E4
Anderson Dr	14 H10	Bog Rd	11 K5
Andrew Cres	13 D12	Bog Rd	7 M4
Annan Ct	7 J1	Bonnyhill Rd	4 A4
Anne Dr	13 D12	Booth Pl	6 H4
Anson Ave	5 E4	Bothkennar Rd	15 K11
Antonine Gdns (1)	8 C5	Boyd La	10 H6
Antonine St	8 C5	Boyd St	10 H6
Arbuthnot St	9 E6	Brackenlees Rd	15 M12
Ardvreck Pl	14 G11	Bradbury St	14 H10
Argyll Ave	11 J6	Braemar Cres	10 J6
Armour Ms	12 B12	Braemar Dr	10 J6
Arnot St	6 J4	Braemar Pl	14 G12
Arnothill	6 G4	Braeview	13 D9
Arnothill Bank (6)	6 H4	Braeview (Laurieston)	7 M3
Arnothill Ct	9 F5	Breton Ct	6 J3
Arnothill Gdns	6 G4	Brodick Pl	4 C4
Arnothill La	9 F5	Brodie St	10 H8
Arnothill Ms	6 G4	Bronte Pl	14 G11
Arran Terr	4 C4	Broomage Ave	12 B11
Arthur's Dr	13 F10	Broomage Bank	12 C10
Ash Gro	13 F11	Broomage Cres	12 B11
Atholl Pl	11 J5	Broomage Dr	12 B11
Auchentyre Pl	14 J11	Broomage Pk	12 C9
Aven Dr	7 M3	Broomhill Ave	12 B9
Avenue, The	15 J10	Broomside Pl	12 B9
Avon Ct	7 J2	Brosdale Ct (4)	6 H2
Baird St	9 D5	Brown St	8 C6
Bairns Ford Ave	10 G7	Bruart Ave	13 F11
Bairns Ford Ct (3)	10 G7	Bruce Cres	14 H11
Bairns Ford Dr	10 G7	Bruce Dr	13 F11
Balfour Cres	12 C10	Bruce St	11 J6
Balmoral Dr	5 E3	Bryce Ave	14 H10
Balmoral Pl	13 E12	Bryson St	10 H6
Balmoral St	5 E3		

Buchanan Ct	10 G8	Castings Rd	11 K6
Burder St	14 G10	Castle Ave	14 J11
Bungalows, The	12 B9	Castle Ct	11 J7
Burns Cres	7 M4	Castle Cres	11 K8
Burnbank Rd	10 H7	Castle Dr (Stenho'muir)	13 F10
Burnbrae Gdns	10 G5	Castle Dr	11 J8
Burnbrae Rd	10 G5	Castle Pl	11 K8
Burnfield Pl	11 K7	Castle Rd	11 J8
Burnfoot La	6 G4	Castlelaurie St	10 J7
Burnhead La	6 J4	Cedar Gro	13 E9
Burnhead Rd	12 C11	Central Bvd	12 B12
Burns Ave	12 C12	Central Dr	13 F11
Burnside Pl	14 H11	Central Pk Ave	12 B12
Burnside Terr	9 E5	Chambers Dr	14 H10
Bute St	10 H6	Chapel Cres	14 H11
Cadell Dr	14 G13	Chapel Dr	13 E11
Calder Pl	7 K1	Chapel La	10 H5
Caledonian Ct	10 J7	Charles Dr	8 C8
Callendar Ave (5)	6 H1	Chestnut Gro	13 F11
Callander Bvd	7 L4	Christie Terr	13 E11
Callander Dr	8 C8	Church Pl	10 H6
Callendar Riggs	6 J4	Church St (Stenho'muir)	13 E10
Callendar Rd	7 K4	Church St (Grahamston)	10 H6
Camelon Rd	9 F5	Church St (Carronshore)	15 J10
Cameron Pl	14 H10	Clanranald Pl	5 F2
Campbell Dr	12 B10	Clarinda Ave	8 B5
Campfield St	10 H6	Clarinda Pl	12 C12
Campie Terr	15 M11	Cluny Dr	13 F12
Canal Rd	9 F6	Clyde Cres	12 B11
Canal St (Camelon)	9 D5	Clyde St	9 E5
Canal St (Grahamston)	10 H7	Cobblebrae Cres	14 H9
Canmore Dr	13 E12	Cochrane Ave	6 H4
Cannons Way	14 G9	Cochrane St	6 H4
Carbrook Terr	12 C11	Cockburn St	6 G4
Carmuirs Ave	8 B6	College Cres	11 K7
Carmuirs Dr	8 B6	Collingwood Ct	9 E5
Carmuirs St	8 B6	Colonsay Terr (3)	6 H2
Carnegie Dr	9 D6	Comely Park Terr	6 H4
Carradale Ave	4 C4	Comely Pl	6 H4
Carrick Pl	4 C4	Conner Ave	10 G8
Carrick Pl (Stenho'muir)	14 G11	Conway Ct	5 F4
Carron Rd	14 G10	Cooperage La	10 G5
Carronbank Ave	14 H10	Corentin Ct	6 J3
Carronbank Ct	14 H10	Coronation Pl	15 M11
Carrongrange Ave	13 E10	Corporation St	6 J4
Carrongrange Gdns	13 E9	Corrie Ave	13 F12
Carrongrange Gro	13 E9	Corrie Ct	11 K6
Carrongrove Ave	14 G10	Corrie Pl	4 D4
Carrongrove Rd	14 G10	Cortachy Ave	14 G11
Carronhall Ave	14 H12	Cottage Cres	9 E5
Carronlea Dr	14 G10	Cow Wynd	6 H4
Carronshore Rd	14 G10	Craigburn Ct (3)	5 F2
Carronside St	14 H9	Craighorn Dr	5 E3
Carronvale Ave	12 D9	Craigie Ct	12 B10
Carronvale Rd	12 C9	Craigievar Ave	14 G11
Carronview	12 D10	Craigleith Ave	5 E2
Castings Ave	10 H7	Craigmillar Pl	13 F12
Castings Ct	10 H7	Cramond Ct (1)	6 H2
Castings Ct	11 L6	Creteil Ct	6 J4
Castings Dr	10 H7	Crathes Ave	14 G12
		Cromwell Dr	7 K4
		Cromwell Rd	7 K4
		Cromwell Rd W	.7 K4
		Cross St	14 H9

Crownest Lo	13 E1…
Cruachan Ct	6 J…
Cuillin Ct	6 J…
Culmore Pl	7 L…
Culvain Pl	7 J…
Culzean Pl	13 F1…
Cumbrae Dr	4 C…
Cunningham Gdns	11 M…
Cunningham Rd	13 F1…
Cuttyfield Pl	14 J1…
Daintree Terr	9 E…
Dalderse Ave	10 H…
Davarr Pl	4 C…
David's Lo	10 H…
Dawson St	10 H…
Denny Rd	12 A…
Derwent Ave	5 F…
Dobbie Ave	12 C…
Dochart Pl	7 H…
Dock St	15 J1…
Dollar Ave	10 G…
Dollar Gdns	10 G…
Dorrator Ct	9 E…
Dorrator Rd	9 E…
Douglas Pl	13 F1…
Doune Cres	14 G…
Drossie Rd	6 G…
Drumlanrig Pl	13 F…
Drummond Pl	5 F…
Dumyat Dr	5 E…
Dunbar Ave	13 F…
Duncan Ave	14 H…
Dundarroch St	12 E…
Dundee Ct (1)	10 G…
Dundee Pl	10 G…
Dunkeld Pl	15 …
Dunning Pl	15 …
Dunnottar Dr	13 F1…
Dunrobin Ave	13 F1…
Dunvegan Ave	13 F1…
Dunvegan Dr	14 …
East Bridge St	6 …
East Dr	12 C…
Eastburn Dr	6 …
Eastburn Tower	6 …
Eastcroft St	12 E…
Edward Ave	13 E…
Edward Pl	15 M…
Elgin Pl	6 …
Elizabeth Ave	12 C1…
Elizabeth Cres	8 E…
Elliot Terr	10 G…
Elm Gro	12 D…
Eriskay Ct	6 …
Estate Ave	7 …
Etna Ct	11 K…
Etna Rd	11 K…
Ettrick Ct	7 K…
Evans St	12 C…
Ewing Ave	10 H…
Ewing Dr	10 H…
Ewing Pl	10 H…
Fairfield Pl	11 …
Fairlie Dr	8 C…
Fairlie Gdns	8 D…
Fairlie St	8 C…
Falcon Dr	12 B1…

irk Rd	6 H2	Glencairn St	8 B5	Holly Ave	13 F11	Lamond View	12 D9	Mansionhouse	9 D5
irk Rd	12 B9	Glenfuir Ct	5 D4	Holyrood Pl	13 E12	Langlees St	14 J9	Rd	
land Pl	13 E12	Glenfuir Rd	9 E5	Hope St	10 H5	Larch Gro	13 F11	Maple Ave	13 F11
m St	14 G9	Glenfuir St	8 C5	Howard St	5 F4	Laurel Ct	8 C6	Margaret Terr	13 E12
quharson	5 F2	Glengarry Cres	5 F1	Howgate	6 H4	Laurieston	7 M4	Mariner Ave	8 B5
ay		Glentye Gdns (5)	5 E3	Howies Pl	4 B4	By-Pass		Mariner Dr	8 C5
guson Dr	14 G13	Glenview Dr	5 F2	Hunter Pl	14 G12	Learmonth St	6 G4	Mariner Gdns	8 C6
n Lea Gro	14 J11	Glynwed Ct	10 J7	Hurworth St	5 F3	Ledmore Pl	7 L1	Mariner Rd	8 C6
dhorn Pl	7 K2	Godfrey Cres	12 C9	Inchkeith Pl	6 H2	Leishman Tower	7 J4	Mariner St	8 B5
stere Ave	6 H3	Gordon Pl	9 E5	Inglis Dr	J10	Lendrick Ave	5 F2	Marmion St	10 H8
arig Ct	13 F12	Gowan Ave	10 H6	Innerpeffray	14 G11	Leven St	10 H8	Marshall La	6 H4
La	12 D9	Gowan La	10 H6	Dr		Lewis Ct	6 H2	Marshall Tower	7 K4
St	10 J6	Gradlon Pl	6 H3	Inver Ct	15 J9	Lime Gro	12 D9	Maryfield Pl	4 B4
ming Dr	14 G11	Graeme Pl	5 E2	Inverary Dr	13 F13	Lime Rd	4 B4	Mather Terr	7 M4
ming Gdns	9 E6	Graham Ave	12 B11	Iona Pl	6 H2	Linlithgow Pl	13 E12	Maxwell Tower	7 K4
bes Ct	11 L6	Grahamsdyke	7 M4	Irving Ct	9 E5	Lint Riggs	10 H5	Mayfield Ms	5 F4
bes Cres	12 D9	St		Islands Cres	6 H2	Lionthorn Ct	5 F2	Meadows, The	14 H10
bes Rd	7 K4	Grahams Rd	10 H6	Jacob Pl	6 H3	Lionthorn Rd	5 E1	Meadow St	6 J4
th Ave	12 B11	Granary Rd	10 G8	James Croft Dr	5 F1	Lismore Ct	6 H2	Meeks Rd	10 H5
thview Ct (4)	5 F2	Granary Sq	10 H7	James St	7 M4	Livingstone	11 L5	Mellock Gdns	5 E2
thview Terr	11 J5	Grange Ave	11 K6	(Laurieston)		Cres		Melrose Pl (12)	6 H4
tuna Ct	6 J4	Grange Dr	11 K6	James St	10 H6	Lochaber Dr	13 E11	Melville La (2)	10 H5
undry Lo	12 B10	Grange View	13 E10	James St	12 C10	Lochgreen Rd	5 E2	Melville St (1)	10 H6
undry St	10 G8	Grangemouth	11 K5	(Larbert)		Lochlands Ave	8 B8	Merchiston Ave	10 G6
nchi Dr	13 F13	Rd		Jamieson Ave	13 E11	Lochlands Lo	8 A7	Merchiston	10 G7
endship	15 J11	Greenbank Ct	5 D4	Jarvie Pl	14 G9	Lochmaben Dr	13 F12	Gdns	
dns		Greenbank Pl	4 D4	John St	10 H7	Lodge Dr	13 F10	Merchiston Rd	10 G6
bisher Ave	9 F5	Greenbank Rd	4 D4	John O'Hara Ct	9 D5	Logie Dr	12 A11	Merchiston Rd	10 G7
irdoch Ave	14 H11	Greenhorns Well	5 F3	Johnston Ave	13 F11	Lomond Cres	13 F11	Merchiston Terr	10 G7
irdoch St	10 G8	Ave (3)		Jones Ave	8 C8	Lomond Dr	14-15 J9	Meredith Dr	13 F11
rden St	10 J5	Grnhorns Well	5 F3	Keir Hardie Ave	7 M3	Longdales Ave	10 G8	Merkland Dr	7 L1
rden Terr	10 J5	Cres (1)		Kemper Ave	6 H3	Longdales	10 G8	Merton Way (6)	5 F3
rrison Pl	10 H5	Greenhorns Well	5 F3	Kenilworth Dr	7 M4	Ct (2)		Middlefield Rd	11 K7
rry Pl	7 J2	Dr (2)		Kenmure Pl	13 F12	Longdales Pl	10 G8	Middlemass Ct	10 H7
rtcows Ave	6 G4	Grenville Ct	9 F5	Kenmuir St	8 A5	Longdales Rd	10 G8	Midthorn Cres	11 L5
rtcows Cres	5 F3	Griffiths St	6 H4	Kennard St	11 J6	Longdyke Pl	14 J12	Mill Ct	14 H11
rtcows Dr	6 G4	Gro Cres (1)	14 G10	Keppock Pl	5 F1	Lorimar Pl	14 H10	Mill Rd	14 H11
rtcows Gdns	6 G4	Halket Cres	14 J10	Kerse Gdns	11 L5	Lorne Gdns	7 M3	Millar Pl	13 F13
rtcows Pl	6 G3	Hallglen Rd	6 H1	Kerse La	10 J5	Lorne Rd	12 C10	Millburn St	11 K5
rtcows Rd	5 F3	Hallglen Terr	6 H1	Kerse Pl	11 K5	MacAdam Pl (1)	9 D6	Millflats St	14 G9
rthill Gdns	6 G4	Hamilton Ave	13 E12	Kilbean Dr	5 E2	MacLaren Ct	13 D10	Mission La (11)	6 H4
rthill La	6 G4	Hamilton Dr	6 G4	Kilbrennan Dr	4 B4	MacLaren Terr	14 G10	Mitchell Pl	5 E2
orge St	10 H5	Hamilton Rd	12 D13	Kildrummy	13 F12	Macfarlane	10 H5	Moffat Ave	14 J11
orge St	12 C11	Hamilton St	8 D6	Ave		Cres		Moncks Rd	7 K4
(arbert)		Harley Ct	10 H8	Kilmory Ct	4 C4	MacIntosh Pl	6 G1	Montfort Pl	6 H3
orge St (1)	7 M4	Harrison Pl	9 E6	Kilns Pl	9 F6	Mackenzie Pl	6 G2	Montgomery	14 H10
(aurieston)		Haugh Gdns	14 H9	Kilns Rd	10 G5	McKell Ct	6 G3	Cres	
rald Terr	13 E11	Haugh St	14 H9	Kincardine Rd	14 J11	McLachlan St	12 C10	Montgomery Dr	14 H10
osongray St	10 G7	Hawley Rd	11 K5	Kings Ct	13 D10	Machrie Ct	4 C4	Montgomery St	11 L5
christ Dr	5 E4	Hawthorn Dr (1)	5 E4	(Larbert)		Macpherson Pl	6 G2	Montgomery	14 H10
fillan Pl	15 J10	Hawthorne Pl	12 D9	Kings Ct (9)	6 H4	Madill Pl	13 F11	Well	
say Ct	6 H2	Hayfield	10 J8	King St	13 E11	Maggie Wood's	5 F4	Morar Dr	15 J9
adstone Rd	13 D11	Hazel Gro	11 K7	(Stenho'muir)		Lo		Morven Ct	7 J2
asgow Rd	8 B6	Hedges, The	9 E5	King St	11 J6	Main St	10 H7	Mossgiel St	8 B5
ebe St	10 H5	Hendry St	10 H7	(Middlefield)		(Bainsford)		Mudale Ct	7 K1
en Brae	6 H3	Heritage Dr	14 G11	Kingseat Pl	5 F3	Main St	13 D10	Muir St	12 D10
en Cres	6 H1	Heugh St	6 G3	Kingsley Ave	13 F11	Main St	9 E5	Muirdyke Ave	14 J11
en Gdns	6 G3	High Pleasance	6 H4	Kinnaird Ave	14 H12	(Camelon)		Muirfield Rd	13 E10
enochil Rd	6 G3	(13)		Kinnaird Dr	13 E11	Main St	14 J11	Muirhall Pl	12 C11
enbank	6 H3	High St	6 H4	Kintyre Pl	4 C4	(Carronshore)		Muirhall Rd	12 C11
enbervie Ave	12 A11	High Station Rd	6 G3	Kirk Ave	13 E11	Main St	12 C10	Muirhead Ave	10 G8
enbervie	12 B11	High Station Rd	6 H3	Kirk Wynd	10 H5	(Larbert)		Muirhead Rd	13 E12
res		Highland Dr	12 C11	Kirkton Pl	14 J11	Majors Lo	6 G4	Mungalend	10 H7
enbervie Dr	12 A11	Hillary Rd	13 D9	Lade Dr	8 C8	Majors Pl	6 G3	Mungalend Ct	10 H7
enbrae St	6 H3	Hillcrest Rd	5 F2	Ladeside Cres	13 E9	Malcolm Dr	13 E12	Mungalhead Rd	10 G7
enburn Rd	7 J1	Hillhead Dr	5 F2	Ladysmill	11 J5	Mandela Ave	10 J7	Munro Gdns	7 M3
		Hillview Rd	12 C11	Ladysgate Ct	14 H11	Manor St	10 H5	Munro St	13 E11
		Hodge St	6 H4	Ladywell Ct	12 A11	Manse Pl	10 H5	Mylne Pl	14 H10

⑫ INDEX TO STREETS - FALKIRK

Myreton Way	5 F3	Queen's Ct	12 D11	Skaithmuir Ave	14 H11	Torridon Ave	14 J9
Nailer Rd	9 E6	Queen's Cres	9 F5	Skaithmuir Cres	14 H11	Torwood Ave	12 B10
Nairn Ct	7 K1	Queen's Dr	9 F5	Skelmorlie Pl	13 F12	Towers Ct	10 H6
Napier Cres	10 G7	Queen's Dr	12 C10	Skythorn	5 E2	Tryst Rd	12 D12
Napier Pl	10 G7	(Larbert)		Way (4)		Tryst Way	13 D11
Neidpath Dr	13 F12	Queen St	11 J5	Slamannan Rd	5 F2	Tulliallan Pl	14 G12
Neilson St	6 H4	Rae Ct	14 J11	Smith St	10 H7	Tummel Pl	13 E11
Nevis Pl	7 J2	Rae St	12 D11	Souter Way	12 C12	Twain Ave	14 G11
Newcarron Ct	10 G8	Raleigh Ct	9 E5	South Bantaskine	6 G3	Union Pl	12 B9
Newcarron Rd	14 G12	Ramsay Ave	7 M3	Ave		Union Rd	9 D5
New Hallglen	7 K2	Randyford Rd	11 K5	South Bantaskine	5 F3	Union St	13 E11
Rd		Randyford St	11 K5	Rd		(Stenho'muir)	
Newhouse Dr	5 E2	Rannoch Pl	13 F11	South Broomage	12 C9	Union St	10 H7
Mewmarket St	10 H5	Redbrae Rd	8 D6	Ave		Universal Rd	11 L7
Newton Ave	15 M11	Redding Rd	7 M3	South Melville	10 H5	Upper	10 H5
North Main St	15 J12	Redpath Dr	14 G13	Ln (3)		Newmarket St	
North St	10 H8	Rennie St	6 G4	South Pleasance	6 H4	Valeview	12 D10
N Distributor Rd	10 J8	River St	14 G9	Ave		Valley View Dr	10 G8
Nursery Rd	5 E4	Robert Bruce	12 B10	South View	13 D9	Valley View Pl	10 G7
Oak Dr	13 D9	Ct		Spinkhill	7 M2	Vicar St	10 H5
Ochil Dr	13 E11	Robert Hardie	12 B10	Spring Bank	11 K5	Victoria Rd	11 J6
Ochil Terr	14 G10	Ct (1)		Gdns		Victoria Rd	12 B9
Ochilview Ct	13 E11	Robertson	12 D10	Springfield Dr	9 F5	(Larbert)	
Ochiltree Terr	8 A5	Ct (2)		Staffa Pl	6 H2	Waddell St	15 J10
Old Bellsdyke	12 A11	Roebuck Pk	13 E10	Stark Ave	9 D5	Waggon Rd	10 H7
Rd		Roman Dr	8 D5	Stenhouse Rd	13 F10	Wall Gdns	8 C6
Old Denny Rd	12 A11	Ronades Rd	10 G7	Steps St	13 E11	Wall St	8 C5
Old Redding Rd	7 M3	Ronald Cres	12 B9	Stewart Rd	11 J5	Wallace Pl	10 J6
Oliver Rd	7 K4	Rose Terr	13 F11	Stirling Rd	8 C8	Wallace St	10 H6
Orchard St	10 J5	Rosebank Ave	9 F5	Strachan St	5 D4	Wardlaw Pl	15 J10
Orkney Pl	6 H2	Rosebank Pl	9 F5	Strathmiglo Pl	13 F12	Waters End	14 H10
Ormond Ct	12 A11	Rosehall Terr	6 H4	Striven Dr	15 J9	Watling Ave	8 C5
Osborne Gdns	5 F3	Ross Cres	8 C5	Summerford	4 D4	Watling Dr	8 D5
Osborne St	5 F3	Roughlands	14 H11	Summerford	4 D4	Watling Gdns	8 D6
Oswald St	6 H4	Cres		Gdns		Watling St	8 C6
Pardovan Pl	9 F6	Roughlands Dr	14 G11	Summerford Rd	5 D4	Watson St	10 H5
Park Ave	13 D10	Roundel The	11 K7	Sunnylaw Pl	5 F3	Watt Gdns	9 E6
Park Ave	7 M4	Rowan Cres	4 A4	Sunnyside Rd	9 F6	Waverley Rd	12 C10
(Laurieston)		Roxburgh Pl	13 F12	Sunnyside St	9 E6	Waverley St	10 H8
Park Ct	14 G9	Russel St	10 H5	Sutton Pk Cres	13 E11	Waverley Terr	12 C10
Park Cres	14 G10	Russell Hill	12 B9	Sutton Pl	11 K5	Webster Ave	14 G12
Park Dr	12 B12	Ct (1)		Swords Way	14 G9	Wee Row	10 H6
Park Dr	12 D10	St Andrews Ct	12 B11	Symington Pl	14 H12	Weir St	10 H5
Park St	10 H5	St Andrews Pl (8)	6 H4	Symon Tower	7 K4	Well Rd	5 F3
Parkfoot Ct	6 H3	St Crispin's Pl	6 H4	Tait Dr	8 C8	Wellside Pl	10 G5
Parkhead Rd	6 H1	St David's Ct	12 B9	Tamfourhill Ave	4 C4	West Bridge St	10 G5
Parkview Ave	5 F2	St George's Ct	12 B9	Tamfourhill Rd	4 C4	West Dr	12 C9
Parkview Ct	9 E5	St Giles Sq	8 B6	Tanner's Rd	10 G5	West Mains Rd	11 M7
Paterson Tower	7 K4	St Giles Way	8 B6	Tantallon Dr	14 G11	Westburn Ave	5 F4
Pembroke St	12 C11	St John's Ave	10 J6	Tanera Ct	6 H2	Western Ave	10 H6
Penders La	10 G5	St John's Ct	10 J6	Tappoch Pl	12 A11	Westerglen Rd	6 G2
Philip Dr	12 D10	St Modans Ct	6 H4	Tay St	15 J9	Westerton Terr	15 J11
Philip St	10 H7	Sainford Cres	14 G9	Taylor's Rd	12 C9	Westfield St	11 K5
Pine Walk	12 D9	Salmon Dr	5 E2	Telford Sq	9 E6	Westminster Pl	13 E12
Pirleyhill Gdns	6 G2	School Walk	13 D11	Teviot St	5 F4	Westray Terr	6 J2
Pleasance	6 H4	Scotia Pl	11 J5	Thistle St	10 J6	Whitegates Pl	4 C4
Pleasance Ct (7)	6 H4	Seafield Ct (2)	5 F2	Thomson Cres	5 E3	Williamson Ave	14 G9
Pleasance Gdns	6 H4	Seaforth Rd	14-15 J9	Thornbridge	11 L5	Williamson Pl	10 J7
Pleasance Rd	6 H4	Seaton Pl	7 J4	Gdns		Williamson St	6 H4
Pleasance Sq	6 H4	Shannon Dr	5 F4	Thornbridge Rd	11 K5	Wilson Ave	8 C5
Portdownie	9 D5	Shiel Gdns	14 J9	Thornbridge Sq	11 L5	Wilson Dr	8 C5
Potter Pl	15 M11	Sherriff La	13 F11	Thorndene Ct (1)	5 F2	Wilson Gdns	8 C6
Pretoria Rd	12 B9	Simpson St	9 E6	Thornhill Ct	11 J6	Wilson Rd	8 C6
Princes St	10 H5	Sinclair Pl	14 G9	Thornhill Rd	10 J6	Windsor Ave	5 E4
Prospect St	9 F5	Sir John	12 B9	Tiree Pl	6 H2	Windsor Cres	5 E4
Prospecthill Rd	6 G2	Graham Ct		Tolbooth St (4)	6 H4	Windsor Dr	5 F4
Quarrolhall	14 H11	Sir William	12 B11	Tophill Entry	9 F5	Windsor Gdns	5 F4
Cres		Wallace Ct		Torlea Pl	12 B11	Windsor Rd	5 E4

Wolfe Rd	7
Woodburn Gdns	11
Woodburn Rd	11
Woodburn St	11
Woodend Walk	6
Woodend Walk	7
Woodlands Cres	6
Woodlands Pl	6
Woodside Ct	6
Woodside Gro	8
Woodside Terr	6
Wooer St (5)	6
Wright St	10
Yardley Pl	14
York Dr	11
York St	11
Zetland Pl	15 M

St	18 J5	Bute Pl	17 F4
St	22 J6	Cairngorm Rd	17 G3
St	19 M4	Campie Pl	20 B9
St	22 J6	Campsie Rd	17 G3
St	19 M4	Canal St	21 E7
St	22 J6	Candie Cres	17 G4
St	19 N4	Candie Rd	22 J6
St	22 J6	Carbrook Pl	17 G4
St	19 N4	Carron Pl	17 F3
St	22 K6	Carronflats Rd	21 G6
St	19 N4	Castleton Cres	17 F4
St	23 K6	Cedar St	17 F5
St	19 N3	Central Ave	17 E4
St	23 L6	Central Dock Rd	21 F7
otsford Dr	18 H4	Central Dock Rd	22 J8
ootsgrange d	21 G6	Charlotte Dundas Ct (1)	17 G4
ootsinch Ct	18 H5	Cheviot Pl	17 G3
ootsinch Rd	18 H5	Chisholm Pl	16 D4
oots Rd	17 F5	Claret Rd	23 L6
ercairney Pl	17 G5	Claret Rd	17 G4
ert Ave	22 H6	Clyde St	20 D7
xander Ave	17 E3	Coll Pl	17 F4
n Ct	21 G7	Compton Rd	17 E3
ond Ct	17 E4	Compressor House Rd	19 K3
ond St	17 E4	Corporation Pl	20 B9
ha St	19 N3	Craigleith Rd	17 F4
berley Path	18 H4	Creteil Pl	21 F6
Ct	17 F3	Crichton Dr	21 G6
an Ct	17 F4	Croftside Ct	17 G4
n Bank Ave	17 G4	Cruachan Pl	18 H3
n Rd	19 M5	Cuillin Pl	17 G3
n St	20 C7	Cultenhove Cres	17 G4
ndale Rd	19 K1	Cunningham St	17 E3
ndhu Gdns	22 H6	Dalgrain Rd	20 D7
moral Rd	19 N4	Dalratho Rd	21 F6
hk St	20 C7	Devon St	20 C7
nkhill Ct	17 F4	Dochart Path	21 F7
rie Pl	17 F3	Dock Rd	21 F7
tery Rd	23 L6	Don St	20 C7
ach Rd	23 K7	Douglas Ave	17 G4
ancross Rd	17 E3	Drummond Pk	17 F4
arcroft Gdns	17 G5	Drummond Pl	21 F6
arcroft Rd	19 L5	Dryburgh Way	18 H4
auly Ct	17 F3	Duke St	22 H6
ech Pl	17 E4	Dundas St	21 E6
l Ct	21 G6	Earl's Rd	20 D6
rryhill Cres	17 G4	Earn Ct	17 F3
nie Pl	20 B8	East Rd	19 L3
ness Rd	18 K5	Eddystone Ct	18 H4
ness Rd	22 H6	Edward Pl	20 B9
ness Rd	21 F7	Elizabeth Ave	17 G5
thkennar Rd	20 A9	Elmbank St	17 E4
vhouse Rd	17 G4	Ettrick Ct	17 G4
vhouse Sq	17 F3	Falkirk Rd	16 B4
e Rd	19 M4	Fendoch Rd	18 H5
avo St	19 N3	Fintry Rd	17 G2
ooke La	17 E3	Flare Rd	19 K3
ooke St	17 E3	Forth St	21 F6
own Ct	17 G5	Forth Terr	21 F6
ace Pl	21 G6	Forties Rd	19 M3
ace Rd	19 N3	Fraser Pl	17 F4
rden Ct	21 G6	Garry Pl	17 G3
chan Pl	17 E3	George St	22 H6
chan Rd	19 M4		
rnbank Rd	17 F4		
nfoot Ct	17 F4		
rns Ave	17 F3		

Glenbervie Rd	18 H4	Mountbatten St	17 E3
Glensburgh Rd	20 C7	Moy Ct	17 F3
Glenside Ct	17 G4	Mull Ct	17 F4
Gort Pl	17 E3	Myreton Rd	17 F4
Grampian Cres	17 G3	Naismith Ct	21 G7
Grange La	21 E7	Nelson Gdns	21 G7
Grange Pl	21 F6	Nelson St	21 G6
Grange Rd	18 H2	Nelson Terr	21 G6
Grangeburn Rd	21 G7	Nevis Pl	17 G3
Grangemouth Rd	19 M3	Newbiggin Rd	17 G4
Green La	21 G6	Newhouse Rd	17 F5
Gunn Rd	17 E3	Newlands Rd	17 E4
Gunner Rd	23 L6	Newton Ave	20 B9
Haig St	17 E4	Newton Rd	20 C8
Haining Pl	22 H6	Ninian Rd	19 N4
Hamilton Rd	17 G4	North Bridge St	21 E7
Hanover Grange	21 F6	North Shore Rd	21 F8
Harris Pl	17 E3	North Shore Rd	22 J9
Harris St	21 G7	Ochil St	17 F5
Hartley Pl	16 D4	Old Refinery Rd	22 J6
Hawthorn St	17 E4	Oldwalls Pl	17 G5
Hazel Rd	17 E4	Oldwalls Rd	23 L6
Henry St	21 G6	Orchard Rd	23 L6
Inchyra Rd	18 H4	Orchard St	17 F5
Islay Ct	17 F3	Oswald Ave	22 H6
Jackson Ave	17 F5	Overton Rd	17 G4
Jinkabout Rd	19 M2	Overton Rd	22 K6
Jura Pl	17 F3	Oxgang Rd	18 H5
Kelvin St	20 C7	Palmer Ct	21 F6
Kenilworth La	17 E3	Panstead St	17 G5
Kenilworth St	17 E3	Paris St	21 G7
Kerse Rd	21 F6	Park Rd	21 F6
Kersiebank Ave	17 G4	Peddie Pl	21 G6
King's Rd	22 H6	Pentland Way	17 G3
Kingseat Ave	17 F4	Poplar St	17 E5
Kinloch Pl	17 G3	Portal Rd	17 E3
La Porte Prec	21 F6	Potter Pl	20 B9
Larch St	17 E4	Powdrake Rd	22 H6
Laurieston Rd	16 C4	Primrose Ave	16 D4
Lawers Pl	17 G3	Princes St	21 G6
Lennox Terr	18 H3	Queen St	22 H6
Library La (1)	21 F7	Quench Rd	19 K3
Lime St	17 E5	Range Rd	23 M6
Loanhead Ave	17 G4	Rannoch Rd	17 F2
Lomond Rd	17 G3	Reddoch Rd	18 H3
Lumley Ct	21 F6	Reddoch Rd	18 J2
Lumley Pl	21 F6	Rifle Rd	23 L6
Lumley St	21 F6	Ritchie Pl	17 E3
Mackenzie Ct	17 E4	Riverside Rd	19 K3
Mackenzie Terr	17 E4	Road 6	19 L5
Magnus Rd	19 M3	Road 7	19 L5
Main Rd	22 J6	Road 9	19 L5
Marmion Rd	17 F3	Road 10	19 L4
Marshall St	21 F6	Road 11	19 L5
Marshall Terr	21 F6	Road 24	18 J4
Maryflats Pl	17 G5	Road 25	18 J4
Melrose Dr	18 H4	Road 27	18 K4
Merrick Rd	18 H3	Road 28	19 K4
Merrick Way	17 G3	Road 29	18 K4
Miller Rd	19 N3	Road 30B	18 K4
Middle St La	21 E7	Road 30C	19 K4
Montgomery St	17 E4	Road 31	19 K4
Morar Ct	17 F3	Road 32	18 K4
Morar Pl	17 F3	Road 33	19 K3
Moray Pl	17 G5	Road 33	19 K4
Moriston Ct	17 G2	Rodney St	17 E4
		Ronaldshay Cr	21 G6

Roxburgh St	21 G6
St Marys Pl	21 G6
Saltcoats Dr	17 G5
Saltcoats Rd	19 J5
Scott St	17 E2
Sealock Ct	17 F3
Sharp Terr	17 E4
Shaw Pl	17 E3
Shiel Ct	17 F2
Sidlaw Pl	17 G3
Skye Ct	17 F4
Smallburn Pl	17 G4
Smiddy Brae	18 H1
South Bridge St	21 E7
South Lumley St	17 E5
South Marshall St	17 F5
South Rd	19 K3
South Shore Rd	21 G7
South Shore Rd	23 K8
Spey Ct	17 F3
Station Rd	21 F7
Stevenston St	17 F3
Strathearn Ct (3)	21 F6
Strowan Rd	18 H5
Strowan Sq	18 H5
Stuart Grove	16 D4
Sunart Pl	17 F2
Swan Pl	17 F3
Talbot St	21 F6
Target Rd	23 L6
Tay St	20 C7
Taylor Ct (2)	21 G7
Tedder St	17 E3
Tenacres Pl	17 G4
Tenacres Rd	19 J5
Thistle Ave	16 D4
Tinto Dr	17 G3
Torwood Ave	17 G4
Troup Ct	21 F6
Tummel Pl	17 G2
Turret Rd	17 F3
Tweed St	20 C7
Union Rd	21 F6
Ure Ct	21 F6
Victoria Rd	21 G6
Wallace Ct	21 F6
Wallace St	21 F6
Wavell St	17 E3
Waverley Cres	17 E3
West Church Dr	20 D7
West Gate Rd	22 J6
Westcliffe Ct (2)	18 H4
Westerton Rd	18 H5
West Mains Rd	16 B5
Wholeflats Rd	18 H2
Wholeflats Rd	19 L2
Wilson St	17 E4
Wood St	17 E4
Woodhill Ct	17 F4
Yarrow Pl	18 H4
York Arcade	21 F7
York La	21 F7
York Sq	20 D6
Zetland Dr	20 C6
Zetland Pl	20 B9

Academy Rd	25 F4	Commissioner St	25 F5
Acre Rd	26 J3	Comrie Terr	25 E3
Amulree Pl	24 C4	Corbiehall	25 D4
Angus St	24 C3	Cowdenhill Rd	26 G4
Antonine Ct	24 C2	Craigfoot Terr	26 G5
Avon Pl	25 E4	Craigview	26 H4
Back Hill (Path)	25 D4	Crawfield La	25 E2
Baker St	25 E3	Crawfield Ave	24 C3
Baptie Pl	25 D2	Crawfield Rd	24 C1
Barony Ct	25 E2	Crosshill Dr	25 E2
Benjamin Dr	24 D2	Cuffabouts	26 J4
Birkhill Cres	25 E3	Darian La	25 E4
Birkhill St	25 E3	Dawson Pl	24 D2
Blair Ave	24 D2	Dean Ct	24 C3
Bog, The	25 F5	Dean Rd	24 D3
Bo'mains Rd	25 D3	Deanburn Wk	24 C3
Bomar Ave	25 F5	Deanburn Gro	24 C3
Bonhard Ct	26 G3	Deanfield Dr	24 D3
Bonhard Way	26 G3	Deanfield Cres	24 D4
Borrowstoun Rd	25 E2	Deanfield Pl	25 D4
Borrowstoun Cres	25 E2	Deanfield Terr	24 D3
Borrowstoun Pl	25 E2	Deanfield Rd	24 C4
Boundary St	26 G5	Deangate Gdns	24 C3
Braefoot Rd	25 F2	Dock St	25 F5
Braehead Gro	25 E4	Doctor Brae	26 G4
Braehead	25 E4	Douglas Rd	25 E3
Brewlands Ave	24 C2	Douglas Dr	25 D3
Bridgeness Cres	26 H4	Douglas Terr	25 E3
Bridgeness La	26 H4	Douglas Pl	25 E3
Bridgeness Rd	26 H5	Dower Cres	26 G5
Buchanan Ct	24 D2	Drum Rd	26 H3
Cadzow Ave	25 E3	Drumacre Rd	26 G3
Cadzow Cres	25 E4	Drumpark Ave	26 G3
Cadzow La	25 E4	Drumside Terr	26 H4
Cairns La	26 G4	Drumview Gdns	25 F2
Carriden Brae	26 J4	Dugald Stewart Ave	25 F4
Carriden Glade	26 J4	Dundas St	25 D4
Carse Vw	24 C2	East Pier St	25 E5
Castlehill	24 C3	Elam Terr	25 D4
Cathrine Gro	25 F2	Erngath Rd	25 F4
Chestnut Gro	24 B2	Ewart Gro	25 E2
Church Wynd	25 E4	Fairspark Terr	24 C2
Church Rd	25 D4	Firwood Dr	24 C2
Clover Pl	24 D2	Foredale Terr	26 J4
Clydesdale St	25 E3	Forthview Cres	24 C3

Fountainpark Cres	26 H4	Kinglass Dr	25 F2
Furnace La (1)	26 H5	Kinglass Park	25 F2
Gauze Pl	25 F3	Kinneil Rd	24 C4
Gauze Rd	25 F3	Kinneil Dr	24 C3
George St	25 E3	Ladywell Vw	24 C2
Gibson's Wynd (6)	25 E5	Liddle Dr	25 D2
Gilburn Rd	24 C3	Links Braes	25 F4
Glen Vw	24 C1	Links Ct	25 F5
Gledhill.Ave	26 J2	Links Rd	25 F5
Glen Ard Vw	26 J3	Links Pl	26 G4
Glenburn Way	24 C2	Linlithgow Rd	25 E4
Graham Cres	26 G4	Little Carriden	26 J2
Grahamsdyke Ave	26 G4	Livingstone Dr	24 C3
Grahamsdyke Rd	26 G4	Loan, The	24 C3
Grahamsdyke Terr	26 G4	Lothian St	25 F3
Grahamsdyke La	26 G4	Lothian Cres	25 F3
Grange Loan	26 G4	Lyon Ct	25 E4
Grangemouth Rd	24 A3	Maidenpark Pl	25 D3
Grangepans	26 G4	Main St	25 F5
Grange Terr	25 F4	Man'o' War Way (1)	26 G5
Green Tree La	24 C2	Marchlands Ave	25 F4
Hadrian Way	26 G3	Marchlands Terr (1)	25 E4
Hamilton Sq	24 C2	Marchlands La	25 F4
Hamilton La (2)	25 E5	Market St (3)	25 E5
Haney's Way	26 G5	Miller Cres	26 J2
Harbour Rd	26 H4	Mingle Pl	25 F3
Hazeldean Ave	24 C2	Muirend St	26 G3
Henry St	25 F2	Muirepark Ct	25 F3
Hillcrest	25 E3	Newtown St	25 E3
Hope St (1)	25 E5	Newtown Cotts	25 E3
Howieson Ave	25 E2	Newtown	25 E3
James Watt Ave	25 F4	North St	25 E5
Jamieson Ave	25 D3	Northbank Dr	25 F2
Jeffrey Bank	25 E4	Northbank Ct	25 F2
Jessfield Pl	25 E2	Northbank Park	25 E2
Kelty Ave	25 F4	Ochilview Rd	25 D3
Kilsland Terr	24 C4	Ochilview Pl	25 D3
Kinacres Gro	26 J4	Ochilview Terr	25 D3
Kinglass Ave	25 F4	Old St Marys La	25 F4
Kinglass Cres	25 F3	Pan Braes	25 D4
		Pan Brae Rd	25 D4
		Park La	26 G4
		Pennelton Pl	25 D2
		Philpingstone La	26 H4

Philpingstone Rd	26 C
Pier Rd	26 H
Pine Grn	24 C
Providence Brae	25 E
Provost Rd	24 E
Quarryknowes, The	25 D
Rattray St	26 G
Redbrae Ave	25 F
Register St (4)	25 E
Richmond Terr	25 D
Ritchie Pl	25 F
Roebuck Pl	24 C
Roman Way	24 C
Run, The	26 H
Salmon Ct	25 E
School Brae	25 E
Scotlands Clo (5)	25 E
Seaview Pl	25 E
Seton Terr	26 G
Shafto Pl	25 E
Snab Brae	24 C
Snab Brae	24 C
Snab La	24 C
S Philpingstone La	26 H
South St	25 E
St John's Way	25 E
Stark's Brae	25 F
Stewart Ave	25 E
Sycamore Ave	24 B
Sylvan Gro	24 C
Thirlestane Pl	26 G
Thirlestane	26 G
Tower Gdns, The (2)	26 H
Union St	25 E
Victoria Pl	26 H
Viewforth	25 F
Viewpark Rd	24 C
Waggon Rd	25 E
Wallace Vw	24 C
Willow Dell	24 C
Woodlands Dr	24 C
Wotherspoon Dr	24 C

INDEX TO STREETS - SOUTH QUEENSFERRY

Almond Gro	33 E2	Echline Ave	32 C3
Arrol Pl	33 E2	Echline Drive	32 B2
Ashburnham Gdns	33 F3	Echline Gdns	32 B3
Ashburnham Lo	33 F3	Echline Grn	32 B3
Ashburnham Rd	33 F2	Echline Gro	32 C3
Atheling Gro	33 E1	Echline Pk	32 B2
Back Braes	32 E3	Echline Pl	32 B2
Bankhead Cotts	33 G2	Echline Rigg	32 C3
Bankhead Gro	33 F3	Echline Terr	32 C2
Bankhead Rd	33 G2	Echline Vw	32 C2
Bellstane	32 D3	Edinburgh Rd	32 E3
Bo'ness Rd	32 B3	Farquhar Terr	32 C3
Brewery Clo (4)	32 D3	Ferryburn	32 E2
Builyeon Rd	32 B2	Ferryburn Grn	32 E2
Burgess Rd	32 E2	Ferry Muir Gate	32 D2
Canmore St	32 D2	Ferrymuir La	32 D2
Carlowrie Ave	33 G1	Ferry Muir Rd	32 D2
Carlowrie Cres	33 G1	Forth Ct (6)	32 E3
Carmelite Rd	32 D2	Forth Pk	33 F2
Catherine Terr	33 E3	Forth Pl	32 B3
Clufflat	32 B4	Forth Terr	33 G2
Clufflat Brae	32 B4	Glebe, The	33 G1
Covenanters La	32 D3	Gote La	32 D3
Dundas Ave	33 E2	Hamilton's Clo (5)	32 D4
East Terr (10)	33 E3	Harbour La	32 D3
Echline	32 B2	Hawes Brae	33 F3

Hawthorn Bank	32 D3	New Halls Rd	33 E3
Henry Ross Pl	32 D3	Ochil Ct	33 E2
High St	32 D3	Old Post Office La (3)	32 D3
Hill Ct (1)	32 D3	Plewland Croft	32 D3
Hillwood Pl	32 D3	Plewlands Pl	32 D2
Hope St	32 D2	Primrose Gdns	33 E2
Hopetoun Rd	32 C3	Priory Gro	32 D2
Hopetoun Rd	32 D3	Provost Milne Gro	33 E1
Hugh Russell Pl	32 D2	Queen Margaret Dr	33 E2
Inchcolm Terr	32 D2	Rosebery Ave	33 E2
Inchgarvie Pk	32 C3	Rosebery Ct	33 E2
Inchkeith Ave	33 E2	Rose La	32 D3
John Mason Ct	32 D3	Rosshill Terr	33 G2
Kempston Gro (2)	33 E2	School La	32 D3
Kempston Pl (1)	33 E2	Scotstoun Ave	32 E1
Kirkliston Rd	32 D2	Scotstoun Grn	32 E2
Lawson Cres	33 E2	Scotstoun Gro	33 E2
Loan, The	32 D3	Scotstoun Pk	32 E1
Loch Pl	32 D3	Shore Rd	32 D4
Loch Rd	32 D3	Smith's Land (7)	32 E3
Long Crook	32 C2	Society Rd	32 B4
Lover's La	33 E3	Sommerville Gdns	33 F1
Main St	33 G1	South Scotstoun	33 E1
Mid Terr (9)	32 E3		
Morison Gdns	32 D3		
Moubray Gro	32 E2		

Springfield Cres	32 B
Springfield Lea	32 B
Springfield Pl	32 B
Springfield Rd	32 B
Springfield Terr	32 B
Springfield Vw	32 B
Springwell Terr	32 D
Standingstone Rd	33 G
Station Rd	32 E
Stewart Clark Ave	33 E
Stewart Terr	32 D
Stoneycroft Rd	32 D
Stoneyflatts	32 C
Stoneyflatts Cres	32 C
Stoneyflatts Pk	32 C
Vennel, The (8)	32 E
Viewforth Bank	32 D
Viewforth Pl	32 D
Viewforth Rd	32 D
Villa Rd	32 D
Walker Drive	32 C
Wellhead Clo	33 F
West Terr (2)	32 D
Whitehead Gro	33 E
William Blake Pl	32 E

'ton Dr	48 B6	Church Wk	50 C9	Greenhill Ct	47 E1	Millar Pl	47 F2	Stoneywood Park (4)	50 A9
lan Cres	50 B11	Claremont St (1)	47 D5	Greenhill Rd	47 E2	Milton Clo	50 B10	Sutherland Dr	48 B7
landale Cotts	46 A1	Conroy Ct	48 C8	Grove St	50 A9	Milton Pl	50 B10	Tarduff Pl	50 A9
loway Cres	46 D5	Cowan St	47 E5	Haughs Way	50 C9	Milton Row	50 B10	Temple Denny Rd	50 B9
nderson Dr	48 B7	Cowden Hill Gdns	47 F4	Hawthorn Dr	50 B10	Montrose Way	46 B4	Thistle Ave	50 B10
nderson Pk Rd	49 D9	Crathie Dr	50 B10	Hayfield Terr	48 C6	Morrison Ave	47 D5	Thorndale Gdns	46 A1
nderson St	47 F4	Creran Dr	46 B5	Haypark Rd	46 B5	Mount Bartholomew	47 E4	Thornton Ave	47 F5
nnet Rd	46 B5	Croftfoot Pl	50 B11	Hazel Cres	50 A10	Murnin Rd	47 E3	Thornton Gdns	47 F5
ntonine Gro	47 D2	Cruikshanks Ct	48 C8	Heatherdale Gdns	48 C6	Myothill Rd	48 B6	Timmons Pl	48 B8
rgyle Path	48 B7	Custonhall Pl	50 B9	Herbertshire St	48 D9	Netherfaulds Dr	48 B8	Town House St	50 C9
shley St	47 D5	Denny Rd	46 C5	High St	47 E4	Nethermains Rd	48 A8	Tygetshaugh Ct	50 B11
trium Pl	47 E2	Denovan Rd	50 B11	Highland Dykes Cres	49 E5	Nisbet Dr	50 B9	Ure Cres	47 E5
von St	50 A11	Dickburn Cres	46 D4	Highland Dykes Dr	49 F5	Northfield Rd	50 A11	Vale Pl	50 C10
vonside Dr	50 B12	Drove Loan	47 D5	Hillcrest Pl	48 B6	N Hair Craigs	48 C6	Vennel, The	50 C9
alfour St	49 D5	Drove Loan	48 C6	Hillhouse Rd	48 C6	Norwood Ave	49 F6	Villabank	50 C9
ankhead Cres	46 B5	Drove Loan Cres	48 C6	Hillview Rd	47 G2	Norwood Ct	49 F6	Walker Dr	46 B4
ankside Ct	50 C9	Drove Rd	48 C6	Hookney Terr	50 A9	Norwood Pl	49 F6	Wallace Cres	50 A9
anton Pl	47 E2	Drummond Pl	49 F5	Hopepark Terr	47 D5	Ochil View	48 A7	Watson Pl	46 A3
arleyhill	47 F4	Dryburgh Ave	50 B9	Hunter Gdns (Denny)	50 B9	Overton Cres	48 B8	Waverley Cres	47 F2
arnego Rd	50 A10	Duke St	50 B9	Hunter Gdns (Bonnybridge)	47 E4	Overton Terr (3)	50 A9	Wellpark Terr	47 E4
axter Cres	48 A8	Duke St	50 A9	Ingleston Ave	50 B11	Paris Ave	48 C8	West Boreland Rd	50 B9
eech Cres	50 A10	Dunbar Gate	50 C10	John Davidson Dr	50 A11	Park Ave	46 C5	Westfield Pl	48 C8
elmont Ave	46 B4	Duncairn Ave	47 D5	Johnston Pl	48 A8	Park St	47 G3	Wheatlands Ave	47 E5
aefaulds Cres	48 B7	Duncan St	47 D4	Jubilee Rd	50 B10	Paterson Pl	47 G5	Wilson Ave	50 B9
onnybridge Rd	46 C4	Duncarron Pl	50 C9	Katrine Pl	46 B5	Pearson Ave	46 B4	Wilson Pl	47 F3
onnyfield Rd	46 D4	Dundaff Ct (2)	48 B8	Kelly Dr	50 C10	Pearson Pl	46 B4	Winchester Ave	49 D9
onnyhill Rd	47 G2	Dunure Cres	47 E4	Kerr Pl	50 B9	Peathill Rd	47 E5	Winchester Ave	50 C10
onnyside Rd	47 F4	Dunure St	47 E4	Kilbirnie Terr	50 B10	Peathill Terr	47 E5	Winchester Ave	50 D10
onnyview Gdns	49 F5	Dunvegan Pl	46 D4	Kirkhall Pl	50 C9	Primrose St (1)	49 F5	Winchester Ct	D10
onnywood Ave	49 F6	Earn Pl	48 B5	Kirkslap	50 C9	Princess St	47 F4	Windsor Dr	50 B10
owling Green Pl (2)	47 D4	East Boreland Pl	49 D9	Knights Way	50 A9	Queens Dr	50 C10	Woodburn Cres	47 D2
aemar Gdns	50 B10	Elmbank Cres	46 B5	Lade Rd	47 E4	Randolph Gdns (3)	48 B8	Woodland Way	48 B6
aes View	48 B7	Endrick Dr	48 C5	Lagta Central	47 E3	Rankin Cres	46 B4		
ewster Pl	50 A9	Fairfield Ave	47 E5	Langhill Pl (1)	48 A8	Reedlands Dr	48 B6		
idge Cres	50 A9	Fairways Pl	49 F6	Larbert Rd	47 E5	Reilly Gdns	47 F2		
idge Pl	50 A9	Falkirk Rd	47 G5	Laurel Ct	50 B10	Reilly Rd	47 F2		
idge St	47 F4	Ferguson Dr	48 B8	Laurel Grove	47 D2	Robertson Ave	49 F5		
oad St	50 C9	Ferguson Gro	49 F5	Laurel Pl	47 D1	Roman Rd	47 E3		
oad St	49 D9	Fleming Ct	48 B7	Laurelbank Ave	47 D2	Rose St (2)	49 F5		
oadside Pl	48 B8	Ford Rd	47 E4	Laxdale Dr	48 B6	Rose Terr	48 B8		
oomhill Pl	50 B11	Foundry Rd	47 F4	Leapark Dr	47 D2	Rulley View	50 A11		
oomhill Rd	47 F3	Gairnoch Wk	48 B8	Leith Pl	48 B6	Russell Pl	46 B4		
oompark Gdns	50 C9	Garvald La (4)	48 B8	Linden Ave	50 A10	Sawers Ave	48 B8		
oomside Rd	47 F2	Garvald Rd	48 B6	Little Denny Rd	48 B8	Sclandersburn Rd	48 A7		
alloch Cres	48 B8	Gateside Ave	47 G5	Loanhead Ave	46 B5	Seabegs Cres	47 E3		
w-Pass Rd	46 C4	Gibbdun Pl	48 C6	Lochhead Ave	48 C8	Seabegs Pl	47 D3		
arronbank	50 C10	Gill Park	50 C9	Lochinver Pl	47 G2	Seabegs Rd	47 E3		
arronside Cres		Glasgow Rd	46 A3	Lochpark Pl	50 C9	Shanks Ave	48 B7		
arronside Pl	50 C10	Glasgow Rd	48 C7	Lochridge Pl	48 B8	Sinclair Cres	48 B8		
astle Cres	50 B9	Glebe St	50 C9	Lomond Way	46 B5	Skene St	47 E5		
astle Terr	50 A9	Glen Terr	48 B8	Loney Cres	48 C7	Smith Pl	48 B8		
astlerankine Rd	48 A8	Glenbo Dr	48 C6	Loudens Wk	50 B12	Solway Dr	48 B6		
nacefield St	49 E5	Glenmore Dr	47 D5	MacLachlan Ave	48 A8	Souillac Dr	48 A8		
nacefield Wood	48 C6	Glenview	46 B4	McTaggart Ave	50 C9	Spence St	49 D5		
nestnut Cres	50 A10	Glenyards Rd	47 E1	Main St	47 F4	Springfield Rd	49 D9		
nurch La	50 B10	Glowrorum Dr	48 C6	Mannfield Ave	47 D3	St Johns Gate (1)	50 A9		
nurch St	47 G2	Godfrey Ave	48 B8	Maple Pl	50 B10	St Johns Gdns	50 A9		
		Gorrie St	50 B9	Margaret Ct	48 C8	St Johns Gro (2)	50 A9		
		Grahamsdyke Cres	47 E2	Margaret Dr	47 E5	Stewart St	47 D4		
		Grahamsdyke Rd	47 E3			Stirling St	50 B12		
		Greenfield St (3)	49 F5			Stirling St	50 C9		

Abbot's Vw 69 K9
Abbotsford Dr 66 E10
Abercairney 60 J5
Cres
Ailsa Ct 61 K5
Ainslie Gdns 69 K9
Airlie Dr 69 K8
Alder Gro 67 F9
Alloway 66 E10
Alyth Dr 65 L7
Anderson Gdns 61 J4
Appin Gro 69 K8
Archibald 64 H7
Russell Ct
Ardmore Dr 65 L7
Arneil Pl 59 H5
Ash Gro 67 F9
Ashley Rd 69 J9
Athol Cres 66 E9
Aven Dr 66 D9
Avondale Rd 69 M9
Avonlea Dr 69 K9
Aylth Dr 65 L7
Back Row 69 K8
Balmoral Gdns 59 H5
Battock Rd 61 J5
Beancross Rd 68 G10
Beech Cres 66 F9
Bellevue 60 J5
Bennet Pl 69 J8
Bethesda Gro 60 J4
Blackmount Terr 61 J4
Blairlodge Ave 64 G6
Blairs Cotts 64 G7
Bo'ness Rd 69 K8
Bog Rd 66 D10
Boyd Street 66 E9
Braemar Gdns 64 H6
Braeside Pl 66 E10
(Laurieston)
Braeside Pl 66 F8
(Redding)
Braeside Pl 63 F6
(R'muirhead)
Braeside 57 B4
Breadalbane Pl 69 K8
Brechin Dr 65 L7
Briar Brae 64 H6
Briardene 66 E9
Brookside 64 H7
Bruce Gdns 64 H6
Buchanan Gdns 67 H8
Burns Cres 66 D10
Burnside Terr 63 F7
Cairneymount 61 L4
Ave
California Rd 60 J4
California Terr 58 D3
Callendar Bvd 66 C9
Callendar Rd 66 C10
Campbell Cres 66 D9
Canal Walk 64 G7
Carhowden Rd 67 F9
Carron Terr 60 J5
Carron Vw 60 J5
Carse Cres 66 E10
Cedar Cres 66 E8
Charlotte St 64 H6
Chrisella Terr 61 L4
Church Rd 58 D3

Colduie Circ 65 K7
Colonsay Ave 67 H8
Comely Pk 60 J5
Comyn Dr 59 G5
Cotton La 66 E9
Craigend Dr 61 L4
Craiglaw Terr 64 H6
Craigs Terr 60 J5
Craigs, The 58 D4
Cranshaws Dr 67 G8
Crawford Dr 58 F5
Cricket Pl 64 G7
Crossgatehead 64 H6
Rd
Dochart Cres 69 K8
Douglas Ave 64 H6
Dovecot Rd 66 E8
Dundas Cres 66 E9
Dundas Rd 66 E9
Dunvegan Pl 65 L7
Eastcroft Dr 69 L8
Ebenezer Pl 58 D3
Eccles Pl 61 L3
Elderslie Dr 58 F5
Elm Dr 66 E8
Epworth Gdns 62 E6
Erbach Ave 67 F10
Ercall Rd 64 J6
Erskine Hill 64 J7
Etive Way 69 L8
Fairhaven Terr 62 E6
Fairways Ave 61 K4
Fir Gro 66 F8
Forest Vw 65 K7
Forfar Pl 65 L7
Forgie Cres 61 L3
Forthview Gdns 64 G6
Forthview Terr 62 F6
Fortingall Cres 69 L8
Fowler Cres 61 L3
Fowler Pl 69 J9
Fullerton Dr 69 J9
Gairloch Cres 67 G8
Garden Terr 66 E8
Gardenhead 69 K8
Gardrum Pl 61 K5
Gardrum Terr 58 D3
George Street 66 D9
Gilston Cres 65 L7
Gilston Pk 69 L8
Glamis Gdns 65 K7
Glendale 64 J6
Glen Avon Pl 61 K5
Glen Lyon Ct 69 L8
Glen Ogle Ct 69 L8
Goodman Pl 60 J5
Grahamsdyke 66 D10
St
Grandsable Rd 67 G9
Grange Pl 64 G7
Grange Rd 69 K10
Grange, The 64 J6
Gray Buchanan 67 H8
Ct
Greenhithe Terr 61 J5
Greenpark Dr 68 J8
Greens, The 61 J4
Greenvale Dr 65 J6
Greenwell Terr 61 J5
Greenwells Dr 65 J6

Haining Gro 61 M3
Haining, The 61 M5
Hamilton Cres 60 J4
Harlington Pl 60 J5
Harlow Ave 64 G7
Harvey Ave 69 K8
Haygate Ave 65 J6
Hayworth Ave 67 F10
Hazelhurst 64 J6
Heather Gro 61 M3
High Rd 61 L3
Hillock Ave 67 G8
Hillside Terr 67 F9
Hillview Rd 64 H6
Holmlea Ave 64 H6
Hornbeam Cres 66 E9
Howff Brae 66 D9
Icehouse Brae 66 E10
Inchyra Rd 68 J10
Inglis Pl 64 J6
Ingram Pl 60 J4
Ivybank Ct 69 J8
James Smith 61 J4
Ave
James Street 66 D9
James Wilson 61 L3
Dr (1)
Jasper Ave 66 E9
Jeffrey Terr 69 K8
Keir Hardie Ave 66 D9
Kendieshill Ave 61 L3
Kenilworth Dr 66 D10
Kenmore Ave 69 K8
Kennard Rd 64 G6
Kestrel Dr 60 J5
Killin Dr 69 L8
Kirkwood Ave 67 G8
Knowehead Rd 67 F8
Langton Rd 66 E9
Lathallan Dr 69 J8
Laurel Gro 66 E8
Laurmont Ct 66 E9
Lawers Cres 69 L8
Lawson Pl 61 L3
Lewis Rd 65 K7
Lime Gro 69 J9
Livingstone Dr 66 D8
Livingstone Terr 63 F7
Lochside Cres 67 F8
Lorne Gdns 66 D9
Lyall Cres 68 J8
Lyness Ct 68 J8
Macarthur Cres 60 J4
Maddiston Rd 64 H6
Main Street 66 H6
(Brightons)
Main Street 69 K8
(Polmont)
Main Street 67 F8
(Redding)
Mamre Dr 58 D3
Mandel Rigg 61 J4
Manor Wynd 61 L4
Maranatha Cres 63 F6
Marchmont Ave 68 J8
Marchmont Ct 69 J8
Mary Square 66 E10
Mary Street 66 D10
Mather Terr 66 D10
Mayfield Rd 67 G8

Meadowbank 64 J7
Meadowbank St 63 F7
Merville Cres 58 D3
Merville Terr 58 D3
Millbank Terr 61 K4
Miller Pk 65 K7
Millfield Dr 68 J8
Montrose Rd 65 L7
Morven Dr 67 H8
Mountjoy Cotts 60 J5
Mossgiel Terr 66 E9
Mumrills Rd 67 G10
Munro Gdns 66 D9
Murray Cres 61 L4
Namayo Ave 66 E9
Netherfield Rd 64 H7
New Hallglen 66 C8
Rd
Newlands Rd 64 G6
Nicolton Ave 61 J5
Nicolton Ct (1) 61 K5
Nicolton Rd 61 K5
Nobel Vw 62 E6
North Ave 65 M6
Oak Bank 66 E8
Oakhill Vw 61 M4
Ochil Dr 61 L3
Old Redding Rd 66 D9
Orchard Gr 61 M3
(Maddiston)
Orchard Gr 69 K8
(Polmont)
Orchard, The 64 H6
Oronsay Ave 61 K4
Overton Cres 62 E7
Park Ave 64 H6
(Brightons)
Park Ave 66 D10
(Laurieston)
Park Cres 66 E9
Park Dr 64 H6
Park Gdns 64 H6
Park Terr 64 H6
Park Vw 64 J6
Parkhall Dr 61 K4
Pine Gro 67 F8
Polmont Ho 64 J7
Gdns
Polmont Pk 68 J9
Polmont Rd 67 F9
Polwarth Ave 64 G6
Poolewe Dr 67 G8
Portree Cres 65 L7
Pretotia Pl 64 J7
Princes Street 58 D3
Quarry Brae 64 J6
Queen's Dr 58 D3
Rainhill Ave 61 J5
Rainhill Ct (1) 61 K5
Ramsay Ave 66 D9
Randolph Cres 64 H7
Redding Rd 67 G9
Redding- 62 E7
muirhead Rd
Richmond Dr 64 G6
Roberts Ave 67 H8
Rodel Dr 65 K7
Roselea Dr 65 J6
Rosemead Terr 58 D3
Salmon Inn Rd 67 H8

Sandy Loan 66 F
Sandyloan Cres 66
School Rd 66
(Laurieston)
School Rd 67
(Redding)
Scott Ave 68
Seaview Terr 61
Shieldhill Rd 62
Silverdale Rd 65
Simpson Dr 61
Skye Dr 65
Smiddy Brae 69
South Ave 61 M
South Brae (2) 61
South Craigs 60
Rd
Spinkhill 66 D
St Catherine 61
St Margaret's 67
Cres
Standrigg Rd 58
Stanley Gdns 61
Station Rd 64
Strang's Pl 58 D
Suilven Heights 66 E
Sunnybrae Terr 61
Sunnyside 59
Cotts
Sunnyside Rd 59
Talman Gdns 69
Taransay Dr 65
Tarbert Pl 65
Tarduff Dr 61
Taymouth Rd 65
Thrums, The 66 E
Tiree Cres 67
Tolsta Cres 65
Toravon Dr 61
Torosay Ave 61
Tudor Ct 67 C
Turret Dr 69 L
Union Pl 64
Vellore Rd 61
Victoria Pl 64
Viewforth Dr 66 F
Waggon Rd 64 C
Wallace Cres 64 G
Wallacelea 60
Wallacestone 59 F
Brae
Ward Ave 67 G
Waverley Pk 63 F
Wesley Pl 62 E
Westquarter 66 F
Ave
Whitesideloan 64
Wholequarter 66 F
Ave
Wholeflats Rd 69 L
Willowbrae 64
Wilson Ave 69 K
Windsor Cres 61
Woodburn Ave 66 F
Woodburn Cres 66 F
Woodlands Dr 64
Woodside Gdns 64
Yew Terr 66
Zetland Dr 66 E
Zetland Terr 69